GLEANINGS

GLEANINGS

A Random Harvest

Selected Writings by

Douglas V. Steere

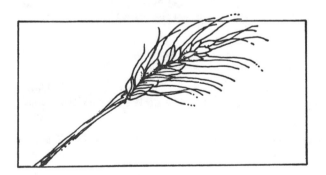

THE UPPER ROOM
Nashville, Tennessee

GLEANINGS

On Listening to Another has been previously published in the United States by Harper & Brothers and has been previously published in England by Allen & Unwin under the title *Where Words Come From*.

"On the Power of Sustained Attention" was previously published as part of a book, *Then and Now*, by the University of Pennsylvania.

Scripture quotations not otherwise identified are from the Revised Standard Version of the Bible, copyrighted 1946, 1952, and © 1971 by the Division of Christian Education, National Council of the Churches of Christ in the United States of America, and are used by permission.

Scripture quotations designated NASB are from the New American Standard Bible, © The Lockman Foundation 1960, 1962, 1963, 1968, 1971, 1972, 1973, 1975, 1977.

Selection taken from Beginning to Pray by Anthony Bloom published and copyright 1984 by Darton, Longman and Todd Ltd and is used by permission of the publisher. Permission to reprint also granted by Paulist Press, publisher in the United States.

The poetry of Evelyn Underhill is reprinted by permission of the Evelyn Underhill Estate, represented by the Tessa Sayle Agency.

Excerpt from *The Faith of a Quaker* by John William Graham is published and copyright 1920 by Cambridge University Press. Reprinted with permission.

Excerpts from Life of Evelyn Underhill by Margaret Cropper are copyright 1958 by Margaret Cropper and are used by permission.

Book and Cover Design: Nancy G. Johnstone
First Printing: November 1986 (5)
Library of Congress Catalog Card Number: 86-50914
ISBN: 0-8358-0543-3
Printed in the United States of America

CONTENTS

.

INTRODUCTION

This small book is not an autobiography, but its chapters have obviously come out of my own life experience. The opening chapter, "Mind Your Call, That's All in All," is the most recently written. It tells very openly a good deal about my own spiritual journey. The thread of my meeting up with Quakerism, in the person of a medical doctor, during my first year as a student at Oxford University in England weaves itself through the years that follow. My inward response to the words of seventeenth-century Quaker Isaac Penington, who wrote in a letter, "There is that near you which will guide you; O wait for it and be sure that you keep to it," spoke so piercingly to my condition that it opened doors. Although six years passed before I actually joined the Society of Friends, I was drawn steadily toward it by its focus upon the Inward Guide and upon the leadings and concerns that come in the Christian pilgrimage.

Later in my life I found Thomas Merton, a Roman Catholic, witnessing in almost identical fashion with the words "You don't have to rush after it. It is there all the time. If you give it a chance, it will make itself known to you." I have found that the precious inward openings that are made known to us are a wonderful beginning, but they need completion. Buried in them is ever so often a "call" in the Christian experience, a call to be minded for things to be done, visits to be made, actions to be taken, and "concerns" to be carried out. The full title of this opening chapter, "Mind Your Call, That's All in All," was taken from a seventeenth-century British Benedictine, Augustine Baker, whose writings were gathered together in a classic volume called *Holy Wisdom*. The calls that I am bidden to "mind" when they have come in my life have required discernment. In this first chapter I have tried to share some of my own experiences that involve both reluctance and yielding.

While several of these chapters contain references to the Society of Friends (Quakers) and their ways, they do not conceal the profound respect for the ecumenical caring that links Friends to the Christian community. We can reach out to support each other only if we know what fresh aspects of the Christian witness can be found in another's response to the piercing love that is at the heart of it all.

The second chapter, "On the Power of Sustained Attention," came to birth in me through the witness of a French heroine of the Second World War, Simone Weil. As a college teacher concerned with kindling students' attention to areas in philosophy and with the centering of interior prayer, I was swept by the profound truth that Simone Weil shared in a small essay suggesting how interconnected all forms of attention really are. I caught her vision of how the sustained gathering and nurturing of our power to open, to focus, and to hold ourselves to whatever we confront actually enables us to be pierced by it. This is true whether what we confront is an insight in philosophy or a luminous season of interior prayer. I was stirred, and I found that her vision opened in me an inward door.

Several years after "On the Power of Sustained Attention" had been published, I was pleasantly surprised to receive a note from a friend of mine, a member of the Princeton Theological Seminary faculty, to ask if I would mind their providing a copy of this message to each of their first-year students as an opener of the inward eye.

"Evelyn Underhill and the Mid-Life Transformation," the third essay, is intended both to express my own debt to her and to draw attention to the variety of mysterious circumstances and ages in which God's deepest breakthroughs often take place. It is interesting to note, for example, that Teresa of Avila's transformation in the sixteenth century came when she was thirty-nine. The great fourteenth-century Flemish spiritual guide, Jan van Ruysbroeck, found his life transformed when he was forty-nine. This essay also shares some insights about Baron von Hügel's spiritual skill in his guidance of Evelyn Underhill during this critical mid-life transformation that took place.

Baron von Hügel and Evelyn Underhill have kindled my spirit for over half a century. I had already been broken open and in search of spiritual company when, a year or so after his death in 1925, I began to read Baron von Hügel and to be deeply touched by him. At that time I knew nothing of the distinguished career of Evelyn Underhill. Later I found that her book *Mysticism*, which appeared in 1911, had become a classic and had lifted her to be a leading authority in interpreting interior religion in Britain. Throughout the First World War, her fine poetry and her smaller books on the spiritual life confirmed her gifts. Although she was part of the Anglican church, that denomination in those years did not seem to meet her needs.

In 1921, ten years after her book on mysticism and an authority on the spiritual life, Eveyln Underhill turned to the great Roman Catholic theologian, Baron von Hügel, who was then almost seventy years old. She begged him to permit her, an Anglican woman in her middle forties, to come under his guidance and to be her spiritual director.

I have tried to describe in this chapter something of the mid-life transformation that took place in Evelyn Underhill and to show how she used these precious years of von Hügel's guidance in the years that followed his death. I first met Evelyn Underhill (Mrs. Stuart Moore) and began to read her books in 1927. I found in her own mid-life transformation and the brilliant harvest that it brought with it a great personal blessing in the years up to her death in 1941.

I hope this essay may encourage its readers to hunt out not only *The Golden Sequence* and the retreat addresses such as *The Fruits of the Spirit*, but very especially to read the classic *The Letters of Evelyn Underhill*, posthumously published in 1943 with a fine introduction by Charles Williams.

The fourth and fifth chapters in this book contain the first and second parts of an address that, in the United States, has had the title of *On Listening to Another* but was called *Where Words Come From* in Britain. Nothing that I have written has seemed to speak to the human condition more tellingly than this address, listed as "On Listening to Another: Part One" and "On Listening to Another: Part Two."

The message was prepared for the annual gathering of British Quakers. The title, *Where Words Come From*, came from an incident that is movingly described in the eighteenth-century journal of the illustrious Quaker John Woolman. Woolman had made a dangerous visit to an Indian village in middle Pennsylvania, and at a religious gathering of the

Indian community, he rose to pray. An interpreter who stood up to render Woolman's words into the Indian language was asked to sit down and let the prayer go untranslated. After the meeting, Chief Papunehang approached Woolman and, through his interpreter, said of the prayer whose English words he had not understood, "I love to feel where words come from."

In an introduction to the British edition of this essay, I said essentially, "If we could learn the art of listening which Chief Papunehang witnessed to, we would be led to the ground of all true conversation, of contemplation, of vocal ministry, and of the deepest level of guidance together with the emergence of 'concerns'—thing to be undertaken." This essay is devoted to an examination of what is involved in listening and in being listened to.

To "love to feel where words come from" and to discover the role this feeling has in the listening that is at the heart of most effective psychotherapy, that marks all genuine spiritual counseling, and that gives us hints of the divine listening that emerges in the deeper levels of prayer is what these two chapters are reaching for.

While this message was originally addressed to Quakers whose public religious services are held on the basis of corporate silence, with oral messages, if any, coming from members who "feel where words come from," the ecumenical exchange that is shared here has over these years been most generously received. Harper and Brothers, who published the first American edition of *On Listening to Another*, later reprinted it in a double volume with *On Beginning from Within*. Its continued relevance in this period when the contemplative life is being so actively explored has drawn it back into print.

The book closes with the sixth chapter, entitled "The Twenty-Third Psalm and the Dialectic of Renewal." It focuses on two phrases in this matchless psalm: "He maketh me to lie down" and "he restoreth my soul." In these two statements, we face not only the experience of being brought low but also the assurance of the shepherd of our lives lifting us in a renewal. Which one of us could grow in the life to which we are called without these patches of brokenness followed by seasons of renewal? W. H. Auden wrote, "It is where we are wounded that God speaks to us." Another contemporary poet dares to say, "Pain is God's megaphone." The wounds and the pain that are referred to here reach far beyond physical disturbances. They search every facet of our pattern of living and caring. They can lead us, all afresh, to experience inwardly what the psalmist promises in his precious words, "He restoreth my soul."

1.

MIND YOUR CALL, THAT'S ALL IN ALL

"Mind Your Call, That's All in All" was an address given in 1982 at Wake Forest University in North Carolina. It was one of half a dozen lectures presented by contemporary interpreters of various aspects of contemplation chosen from different parts of the country.

I grew up in the state of Michigan and my religious experience as a boy was not untypical of many young Protestants. When I was about fourteen, I was deeply moved by a young evangelist who gave me a sense of how God had singled me out and loved me. I joined the Methodist church, transferred to the Presbyterian church to save a mile of walking each Sunday, and finally settled at the Evangelical and Reformed church. This decision was made not on any theological grounds but because they badly needed the help of my slide trombone in their Sunday school orchestra!

I studied agriculture at what was then Michigan Agricultural College, now Michigan State University, with potatoes as my specialty. At the end of the third year I found myself weary with activities, so my dearest friend and I decided to take a year off. At the age of nineteen I taught chemistry and agriculture at a vigorous high school in Onaway, located in what might be classified as one of northern Michigan's least developed counties. In addition to teaching, I traveled with the county agriculture agent at night once or twice a week to remote parts of the county for meetings with farmers. The teaching and the work with the farmers went amazingly well, but as the year went on, I had a deep inner sense of guidance that this work was not what I was put on earth for.

I returned to the college for my senior year. In the course of that year I had the close friendship of a gifted member of the faculty. I never had a course with him but, on more than a few nights, we talked far into the small hours. In this period I had deep doubts about myself, but he confirmed the deepest thing in me. I had worked my way through college, but with his encouragement I borrowed a thousand dollars to go to Harvard to study philosophy.

In my college years the church had meant something to me. I suspect that my eagerness to study philosophy came from a longing to find a frame for the inner guidance that had so decisively drawn me away from the agricultural occupation for which I was well trained. Instead of giving me this longed-for frame for my faith and experience, however, my study of philosophy wiped out what little faith I had. By spring of my first year at Harvard, I touched bottom and saw little to live for.

I remember a Chinese student at that time telling me of his own earlier conversion in his native city of Canton. Like most of his fellow students, he was lured to communism, but he had also felt a drawing toward the Christian way. He told me that early one morning he wakened suddenly and saw Jesus Christ standing beside his bed. Jesus had reached down and taken him by the hand, literally lifting him out of bed. He knew instantly that he must renounce communism and follow Jesus. I felt wistful and wished that I could have such a decisive experience.

It was at this lowest time in the spring of 1924 that I met some fellow students to whom silent prayer and an inner sense of the guidance of God was very real. While I never joined their official group, several of them at the Episcopal Theological School in Cambridge invited me to meet with them. It was in these noonday sessions of silence that I began to pray again. By the end of this first Harvard year, I had been inwardly renewed in my faith. The renewal had come to me through silent prayer, into which I could bring anything. The sense of God's guidance grew in me as I tried to be faithful to what I came to understand during these seasons of prayer.

In the spring of my second year at Harvard, I decided to take the full battery of four comprehensive examinations that, if I passed, would clear the way for writing a doctoral thesis in philosophy. There was no compulsion to take these tests at this time. The previous autumn I had been awarded a Rhodes Scholarship for three years of study at Oxford University, where I could go on in philosophy. Coming to Harvard with no undergraduate preparation in the field of philosophy, I had only a bare minimum of courses with which to tackle these examinations. But I had signed the papers to take them. The night before the ordeal of the first examination came, I had a crisis. I was deluged with all of the reasons for postponement. How much better to wait until I had two or three years of preparation at Oxford. How stupid to risk the humiliation of failing them if I took them now. I was sorely tempted to cancel out the next morning as a certain percentage of annual candidates were reported always to do.

That night at two o'clock, I knelt in prayer and asked for guidance. I stayed on my knees for half an hour and I felt the clear leading to take the tests—to go into each one of the four with a quiet mind, to write what I could, and to accept without a quiver the outcome, whatever it might turn out to be. I went to bed with a quiet mind, slept soundly for four hours, and got up in the morning with an easy heart. I wrote the four three-hour papers during the next days with a steadiness and an ease that never deserted me. Some weeks later I was notified that I had passed the comprehensives. Only an acceptable thesis and the language tests remained to fulfill the requirements for the doctorate.

It was in England that I first discovered, to my surprise, that something known as Quakerism was centered in the guidance of the inward Christ and was not simply a chapter in seventeenth-century history but was actively alive today. I had strained my back in rowing at Oriel College and was directed to a well-known Oxford doctor named Henry Gillett, who turned out to be a Quaker. We struck up a friendship that went on through the rest of my time at Oxford and beyond. A year or so later, with a reading party of other Oxford students, I attended an hour's silent Quaker meeting at Old Jordan's Hostel. It was there that I first felt the power of Christ's indwelling spirit sweep through me and that I came to experience what the Quakers call a "gathered" or a "covered" meeting. It was through Dr. Gillett that I was invited to spend the night with Rufus Jones at Haverford College when, after spending the summer in America, I was on my way back to England for my third year at Oxford. And it was from this visit that I was invited to join Rufus Jones a year later as his junior colleague and to teach philosophy at Haverford College for what turned out to be the rest of my professional life.

With this growing hunger to understand better the inner experience of divine guidance that had come to me, I decided in my final year at Oxford (1927-28) to bury myself in the writing of the Roman Catholic philosopher and theologian, Baron von Hügel, and to prepare myself to write a doctoral thesis for Harvard on his thought. In the course of that year, only two years after the baron's death in 1925, I came to know a number of his closest friends. Professor Percy Gardiner, the baron's literary executor, generously gave me access to von Hügel's unpublished papers.

In the course of these visits I came to know Evelyn Underhill. Although she was and remained an Anglican, for the last three years of von Hügel's life she had been under his spiritual direction, and her life had been immeasurably deepened by him. In the next decade her books were treasures that I especially prized.

In her earlier books on mysticism, she had some plain words for the universality of the contemplative and mystical dimension in the breast of every person. There she says, "Ordinary contemplation . . . is possible to all men: without it, they are not wholly conscious, nor wholly alive."[1] Without any radical discontinuity, she connects this contemplation with the highest glimpses the great mystics report of the ultimate togetherness: "The spring of the amazing energy which enables the great mystic to rise to freedom and dominate his world, is latent in all of us; an integral part of our humanity."[2]

On a visit I made at her invitation to her home in London, I asked if she had herself experienced the inward wave of love that had been witnessed to by many of these classic figures among the mystics that she wrote about. She was a slight figure of a woman with sparkling eyes, and her reply to me was honest and direct. Looking directly at me, she said that no, she had not had the major experiences that marked the great mystics, but she *had* experienced what it was to have "a slowing down." This and no more was her answer. In the fifteen years of her life that followed von Hügel's death, she gave much-sought-after retreats in the ancient Pleshey Retreat House in Essex. Her addresses there contained the kernels of the books that appeared one after another in those productive closing years of her life. These books and her letters, the latter posthumously published, are among the treasures we have to draw upon to help us better understand the guiding power of God working within our lives.

I came to Haverford College in 1928 not as one transformed by a Damascus Road or an Aldersgate experience but rather as one who knew something about what a contemporary Quaker writer, Elizabeth Vining, called "minor ecstasies." I had begun a journey and am still on the way. My life has not been a once-born or twice-born, but, I hope, one that goes on experiencing a continuous conversion. I found Haverford College a congenial atmosphere for continuing this journey. In my first semester at Haverford, I persuaded Rufus Jones to give a small seminar on Meister Eckhart, who was a great passion of his. The half dozen of us who were in the seminar, including Howard Thurman, found ourselves searched to the core by Eckhart's depiction of the transforming power of Christ within.

The following year, 1929, my wife Dorothy Steere joined me at Haverford. Although not at that time members of the Society of Friends, we were included in a group of Quakers who, in 1930, established a small center for study and contemplation that was called Pendle Hill, located some ten miles from Haverford. Dr. Henry Hodgkin, a British Quaker medical doctor and religious statesman who had spent twenty-five years in China, responded to our call to become the first director of Pendle Hill. I found in him the greatest Christian I had ever come to know intimately. Few persons knew the hidden roots of Henry Hodgkin's spiritual life. Early each morning he spent at least an hour in his silent time of inward listening in prayer, his reading in a devotional classic, and his pouring out in a secret daybook the insights and concerns that had come to him. He spoke often of the inward tendering. At the end of two swift years he was fatally stricken with cancer, but in these two critical years he had launched Pendle Hill, this precious island of spiritual and social guidance that has touched the lives of so many persons in the past half century of its existence.

Dorothy and I were deeply moved by the corporate Quaker

meetings on the basis of silence. We found that, in the climate of this group silence, the interior presence of Christ moved within us and centered and renewed our dispersed lives and, from time to time, laid on us things to be done. In 1930 we were invited to join with half a dozen others in opening a beautiful old meetinghouse located out in the country some four miles from Haverford. It had been built in 1718 but had been closed in about 1880, as its members had nearly all moved away. Now with motor cars more common, Radnor Meeting became accessible again. We gathered each Sunday morning with heating supplied by an old potbellied stove and the lighting by candles and oil lamps.

In these same years I was drawn into the work of the American Friends Service Committee. We were especially concerned for the coal fields of Western Pennsylvania and of West Virginia at this time, where, due to the depression and closing of the mines, literal starvation was taking place. Local, county, and state funds were exhausted, and no federal aid was in existence. We were feeding children in that whole area. In order to give some Christmas leave to our regular team of workers there, I took a small group of Quaker students from Haverford College into Logan, West Virginia, to carry on the feeding over the holidays. I saw what it meant for unemployed miners and their families to stay alive from picking over garbage dumps or gathering greens from the weeds.

During the first four years at Haverford, Dorothy and I were reluctant to join the Quakers. Neither of us was basically a joiner in our adulthood and now, with the expectation of a child and with duties that were mounting for both of us, we continued to hold back. In the spring of 1932, we read John Woolman's *Journal*. He was a Mt. Holly, New Jersey, Quaker who lived from 1720-72. From his mid-twenties until his death, he found the concern and the time to help end the holding of slaves among the Society of Friends. In this moving journal, we found that our last hesitations about joining the Society of Friends had quietly melted away. For in Woolman we discovered someone who lived in the world as we did; who was married and had a family as we did; who supported his family and his journeys by his own labor as we meant to do. In Woolman we found a person in whom the inward tendering and the concern for his fellows that the Guide had laid upon him were brought together and carried out. We both agreed that, with all of our frailties, the time had come for us to throw in our lot with the Quakers. We applied for membership and were admitted.

Thirty years later, looking back at our life in the 1960s, which included close relationships with the Roman Catholics, our presence at three sessions of the Vatican Council II, and the founding, with Father Godfrey Diekmann, of the Ecumenical Institute for Spirituality, it is of interest to see how the Inward Guide often prepares us far in advance for work that will be laid upon us later. In 1931, Dr. Maria Schlüter-Hermkes, a distinguished Roman Catholic scholar, was brought to this country by the Carl Schurz Foundation to lecture on several of the great Roman Catholic saints. I met her and found much common ground. Since I knew German, she encouraged me to come to Germany on my first sabbatical leave from Haverford and promised that she and her husband would open to me the world of German Roman Catholic spirituality.

Haverford College generously gave me this leave in 1933-34, and with arrangements made for Dorothy to join me in midyear, I crossed to Germany in August 1933, the first year Hitler was in power. Through the husband of Dr. Schlüter-Hermkes, I was invited to spend a month in the great Benedictine monastery of Maria Laach in the Andernach area. In due time I was taken to meet Maria Laach's famous Abbot Herwegen. With some pleasant chuckles, he chided me a little for coming to a Benedictine monastery for a month of personal retreat and pointed out that the Benedictine Order had little faith in private retreats and private piety. For them, salvation came rather from being a part of a family or a community and not by any private nurturing! Nevertheless, he sent to me, as a companion and spiritual guide, Father Damasus Winzen, a monk of almost exactly my own age.

How little at the time did I realize that Damasus Winzen was to become one of the most beloved friends of my life! He suggested that we read and discuss together Swedish Lutheran professor Nygren's *Agape and Eros*, which had only recently been translated from the Swedish. The book's overwhelming accent on God's undeserved grace and love that is poured out on us searched me deeply during these days. One afternoon when I was out walking, I saw a peasant farmer with a great sling of wheat tied over his left shoulder. Reaching his right hand deep into this sling, he flung the wheat seed out recklessly onto the harrowed land as he moved across the field. There was no skimping, no measuring, no looking back, only the wanton forward thrusting of his gait as he marched across the field. I was overwhelmed with its likeness to God's grace. In the same moment I was swept with an overpowering wave of love for my mother, who through all these years had poured out on me that very kind of caring. Our family had never been very demonstrative; we were not given to express our affections very openly. But now I turned my steps back to the monastery and went to my room. I wrote my mother a love letter in which I broke over all boundaries and told her how much I loved her and that suddenly I had come to realize how little I had thanked her or shown what that love of hers had meant to me. Something broke in me at that point, and I began to see and feel that at the bottom of it all, it is love that matters, love that opens the way. I began to realize that Augustine expresses it all when he says, "We come to God by love and not by navigation" (that is, not by detailed spiritual charts). Now I could understand in a new way what the old nineteenth-century Scot, George Macdonald, meant when he wrote, "Pray to the God of sparrows, rabbits, and men, who never leaves anyone out of his ken."

Strangely enough, Father Damasus came to the United States two years later on a commission to see where Maria Laach might be relocated in this country should the Nazi persecution drive the monks out of Germany. This never occurred, but Father Damasus stayed on here for the rest of his life, and our friendship kept deepening with the years. In 1951 he founded a vigorous new monastery called Mt. Saviour that lies between Elmira and Corning in the state of New York. Forty men had joined it before he passed away in 1971. Only a few months before his death, Father Damasus expressed with great power and clarity the heart of my own experience of that peasant farmer almost forty years before. He told a companion, "When I look back upon the seventy years of my own life, I see quite clearly that I owe my present inner happiness, my peace, my confidence, and my joy essentially to one fact: I am certain that I am infinitely loved by God."

In that first sabbatical year of mine, my scholarly friend, Maria Schlüter-Hermkes, more than fulfilled her promise to open the way for me to come to know some of the great German spirits in the Roman Catholic community. I was able to meet Alois Dempf, Theodore Haecker, Dr. Scheningh, who was the editor of *Hochland*, the finest Catholic journal in the country, and Eckhart scholar Joseph Bernhart. When I got to Berlin I was able not only to meet Romano Guardini, who, in the German Catholic world, scarcely had an equal in mind or spirit in that period, but to have evenings with him in his home at Eichkampf. That year I learned Danish and translated Søren Kierkegaard's *Purity of Heart*.

In the autumn and spring of 1936-37, I found an old lady who lived in Solebury, Pennsylvania, an hour's journey from Haverford, who took me in and gave me board and room on weekends and let me have the use of a folding table in her ancient woodshed. There I wrote my first book for the Hazen series, *Prayer and Worship*. Twenty-five years later I enlarged upon it at the Methodists' urging. Under the title *Dimensions of Prayer*, it became their mission study book for the year 1962. In this revised book on prayer I especially accented the importance of the way that I enter prayer. I am sympathetic to the use of any meditation practices that can still the mind and relax the body, but they are vestibule exercises. When I am ready to enter prayer, I feel it wise not to enter it in a state of mind in which I project the prayer, in which I take the initiative of cranking it up. Instead, it makes such a difference if I enter prayer in awesome awareness that I am beseiged by and immersed in a love that is utterly without qualification. It is not that God loves me *if*, but simply that God loves me. Von Hügel's word is, "It is God who wakes and God who slakes our thirst."

Meister Eckhart in one of his eloquent sermons gives his own witness to this operation of the divine initiative: "God is foolishly in love with us, it seems he has forgotten heaven and earth and all his happiness and deity, his entire business seems with me alone, to give me everything to comfort me; he gives it to me suddenly, he gives it to me wholly, he gives it to me perfect, he gives it all the time and he gives it to all creatures."[3] Eckhart pauses, and then asks, "Why are you not aware of it?" He answers his own question: "Because you are not at home in the soul's inmost center."

Bernard of Clairvaux, in the twelfth century, has a lovely passage in one of his sermons to his monks in which he deals with eager beaver brothers who try to creep into the chapel before the Cistercian company's appointed hour of morning gathering at 3:15 A.M., hoping perhaps that they might sometime manage to get into their places before God came! "Do you awake?" Bernard asks. "Well He, too, is awake; if you rise in the night time; if you anticipate to your utmost your earliest awaking; you will find Him awaking. You will never anticipate His awakeness. In such an intercourse, you will always be rash if you attribute any priority or predominant share to yourself. For He loves both more than you and before you love at all."[4]

It is hard for me to underline sufficiently what a difference it makes to enter prayer with a deep consciousness of this divine initiative—to be conscious that long before I make my response in prayer at all, something immensely costly and penetrating has been going on; that it continues during my prayer; and that it continues to undergird my very life when I have turned from conscious acts of prayer to my other tasks of the day. This, and nothing short of this, gives prayer its true setting. "Prayer is a response to God's Isness" is another way to put it. My prayer did not initiate this encompassing love. This love has been like a poultice laid over me and laid over the world for its healing long before I came on the scene. When I pray I simply enter into an ongoing stream, and my act of prayer, precious and important as it truly is, is swept up into something infinitely more vast where it is cleansed for use.

I will not attempt here to go beyond naming the familiar sequence of praying that is stirred by this realization of God's initiative. There is adoration and thankfulness, contrition and yielding, petition and intercession, and a listening for the biddings laid upon us by the Inward Guide for taking part in the interpersonal life of our time. Yet all of these voluntary aspects of my prayer are greatly affected by the door through which they enter into the presence of the divine. Paul Claudel, the French poet, says, "All prayer is simply thankfulness that God is!"

My own life in these years was being blessed by the weekly hour of corporate prayer in the little, steadily growing Radner Meeting. I must say something about this experience or I cannot explain the Quaker union of the guiding hand of God in our lives that the meeting renews and the further dimension of holy nudges and concerns that are laid on us there for service far beyond the Meeting doors.

Alexander Parker, a trusted friend of George Fox, has brief advice for the conduct of such a corporate meeting for worship:

> The first that enters into the place of your meeting, be not careless nor wander up and down either in body or mind, but innocently sit down in some place and turn in thy mind to the Light, and wait upon God simply as if none were present but the Lord, and here thou art strong. When the next come in, let them in simplicity at heart sit down and turn to the same Light, and wait in the Spirit, and so all the rest coming in the fear of the Lord, sit down in pure stillness and silence of all flesh, and wait in the Light. A few that are thus gathered by the arm of the Lord into the unity of the Spirit, this is a sweet and precious meeting in which all are met in the Lord.[5]

There is a story about strangers getting into such a silent meeting by mistake and sitting for an hour in bewildered expectancy of hearing a sermon. It tells of one of these visitors turning to his companion at the close of the hour when all rose to leave and saying, "Doesn't this beat the devil." An old Quaker who overheard the remark leaned over to him and said, "Friend, that is exactly what the meeting is for."

I should add that there is always complete liberty on the part of either men or women to share briefly any message that might be given to them for the meeting, although it is not uncommon for the hour to pass in complete silence. After some years of experience in these meetings for worship I was asked to write down what the meeting meant to me. I am taking the liberty here of including two paragraphs from my response to this request.

The meeting for worship has sent tears down my cheeks. It has given me specific things to be done and the strength to undertake them. It has, on a few occasions, laid on my heart rimless concerns whose precise structure and whose outcome I could not foresee and kept them before me until they came to some degree of clarity. It has called me into the intercessory chain gang to pray for other people and for situations where the need was urgent. It has changed my mind when I did not mean to change it. It has firmed me up when I might have yielded. It has rested me. It has upset my sluggish rest. It has helped prepare me to live. It has fortified me in knowing that my ashes will eventually lie in the earth only a couple of hundred feet from where I am sitting at Radner Meeting and has helped me to feel the presence of the One who can bear me now and bear me then.

It has scarified me and broken down the hull of my life and shown me how I might live. It has warned me that I am too cowardly to live that way, but reminded me for good measure that it is not what I give that makes me suffer but what I hold back! It has comforted and quieted me when I was torn and hurt, and it has dug up the garden of my soul when I thought the present produce was all I could manage. In it I have physically slept and again I have been terribly awake. In it my mind has wandered like a hummingbird on holiday and yet in it I have felt moments of intensity and of concentration and awareness that have shown me what life could be like.

In a far more cultivated fashion, Donald Court, a highly esteemed British Quaker doctor and professor of public medicine at the University of Leeds, speaks of both the daily times of stillness and the weekly corporate meeting for worship. Of them he says: "These are times to reach down to a level where I can see myself and my work straight, where that strength we call love can break through my anxiety and teach me how to respond instead of to react . . . , how to open the road to a spirit blocked by busyness, self-importance, self-indulgence, self-pity, depression and despair. I could not have coped, perhaps even survived the last 35 years without the meeting for worship."[6] In Donald Court's exposure of the healing return to wholeness that has come to him in the corporate silent meeting, he is describing the gathering power of the Inward Christ.

In these nurturing seasons of corporate waiting in the meeting for worship from time to time, as I mentioned earlier, we seem to be taken beyond ourselves and, instead of *praying*, we seem to be prayed *in*. Friends call such an occasion a "gathered" or a "covered" meeting. An old Russian Orthodox saint of the ancient past was speaking about such a moment in private prayer in his word, "When the Holy Spirit speaks, *stop* praying!"

I want to share with you a scene from a little book called *Beginning to Pray*, written by the London Russian Orthodox archbishop Anthony Bloom. Bloom describes these moments where effortful prayer is meant to stop and where the gift of the effortless sense of God's presence appears:

> About twenty years ago soon after my ordination, I was sent before Christmas to an old people's home. There lived an old lady . . . who came to see me after my first celebration and said "Father, I would like to have advice about prayer." So I said "Oh yes, ask So-and-so." She said "All these years I have been asking people who are reputed to know about prayer, and they have never given me a sensible reply, so I thought that as you probably know nothing, you may by chance blunder out the right thing." That was a very encouraging situation! And so I said "What is your problem?" The old lady said "These fourteen years I have been praying the Jesus Prayer almost continually, and never have I perceived God's presence at all." . . . I said "If you speak all the time, you don't give God a chance to place a word in." She said "What shall I do?" I said "Go to your room after breakfast, put it right. . . . Light your little lamp before the ikon that you have and first of all take stock of your room. Just sit, look round, and try to see where you live, because I am sure that if you have prayed all these fourteen years it is a long time since you have seen your room. And then take your knitting and for fifteen minutes knit before the face of God, but I forbid you to say one word of prayer. You just knit and try to enjoy the peace of your room."
>
> She didn't think it was very pious advice but she took it. After a while she came to see me and said "You know, it

works." I said "What works, what happens?" because I was very curious to know how my advice worked. And she said "I did just what you advised me to do. I got up, washed, put my room right, had breakfast, came back, made sure that nothing was there that would worry me, and then I settled in my armchair and thought 'Oh how nice, I have fifteen minutes during which I can do nothing without being guilty!' and I looked round and for the first time after years I thought, 'Goodness what a nice room I live in. . . .' " Then she said, "I felt so quiet because the room was so peaceful. There was a clock ticking but it didn't disturb the silence, its ticking just underlined the fact that everything was so still and after a while I remembered that I must knit before the face of God, and so I began to knit. And I became more and more aware of the silence. The needles hit the armrest of my chair, the clock was ticking peacefully, there was nothing to bother about, I had no need of straining myself, and then I perceived that this silence was not simply an absence . . . of something but presence of something. The silence had a density, a richness, and it began to pervade me. The silence around began to come and meet the silence in me." . . . "All of a sudden I perceived that the silence was a presence. At the heart of the silence there was Him who is all stillness, all peace, all poise."[7]

In *The Varieties of Religious Experience*, William James writes, "Our normal waking consciousness, rational consciousness as we call it, is but one special type of consciousness, whilst all about it, parted from it by the filmiest of screens, there lie potential forms of consciousness entirely different. We may go through life without suspecting their existence; but apply the requisite stimulus, and at a touch they are there."[8] William Blake says, "If the doors of perception were cleansed, everything would appear to man as it is, infinite."

Whether it is on another level of consciousness or whether the doors of perception are secretly cleansed, in these moments of a gathered meeting, the Quaker experience is that with this gift of the presence and with its accompanying sense of deepened solidarity with our fellow creatures, there seem to come now to this person and now to that the holy nudges, the tasks, the concerns that need to be undertaken. These concerns can and do, of course, come in any situation, but the meeting for worship has been found to be of special importance in initiating and in dealing with them. These seeds of concerns are not put there on an ornamental basis. They are secretly given to us to be worked over and to be acted upon. The price of neglect or refusal of such leadings may not be small.

Archbishop William Temple in his great Gifford Lectures, *Nature, Man and God*, suggests that the eternal nature of God is unchanging but that God's strategy is infinitely variable. The implication of this suggestion is that if, when a task is laid on me from within, I shun it or neglect it, God's whole strategy may have to be changed! In other words, it is being suggested that my response to the holy nudge may have cosmic consequences!

The meeting for worship is often spoken of as being built on the basis of silence and obedience. Thomas Mann, in an address at the Library of Congress, once confided, "Were I to determine what I personally mean by religiousness, I should say it is attentiveness and obedience." Without attentiveness in both private and public worship, there can be only a confirmation of the African proverb that says, "When God speaks he does not wake up the sleeper." But unless this precious attentiveness is linked to obedience, the deeper bond is missing. To come near to God is to change, and unless there is obedience, a change of will and a willingness to open the sealed orders and seek to carry them out, I have failed the divine love that bid me to join God.

Romano Guardini first urged me to read the books of a contemporary Swiss woman medical doctor and Christian mystic who wrote under the name of Adrienne von Speyr. In one of her books, *The Word*, she says, "To receive God means to make room for God, whatever he may be or bring. It may be only a call to be prepared, a vague indefinite and indefinable demand, or on the other hand, it may be a visible or intelligible task; it may be a single action, or just one word spoken . . . once open to the Light man may ask God to claim him more essentially and more profoundly. But on one condition only, on condition that he does not refuse the first small act that God demands of him."⁹ She might well have gone on to add to this "first small act"—and the countless others that are to follow.

Three strong voices from the seventeenth century underline both the Guide's laying on us specific things to be done and the promptness required in carrying out these inward directions. Francis de Sales goes so far as to define devotion in terms of the swiftness with which we respond to the inner bidding. "Devotion is the promptitude, fervor, affection and agility which we show in the service of God." He extends this with "God requires a faithful fulfillment of the merest trifle given us to do, rather than the most ardent aspiration to things to which we are not called." In Britain a few decades later, the beloved seventeenth-century Quaker, Isaac Penington, wrote a line that I have always treasured: "There is that near you which will guide you. O wait for it and be sure that ye keep to it." Augustine Baker, the seventeenth-century Benedictine who wrote the classic *Holy Wisdom*, put it all in seven words, "Mind your call, that's all in all."

This dimension of obedience, this "mind your call" and the following of the Guide, is such a vital part of the Quaker religious experience that I am going to cite swiftly two classical examples and then conclude with some personal witness to both this obedience dimension and the visible and invisible barriers that confront it. Nerius Mendenhall was a Quaker who, with his family, headed the New Garden Friends Boarding School in Greensboro, North Carolina, in the years that led up to the American Civil War. As the inevitability of the war and of North Carolina's being squarely united with the Confederate cause of breaking with the Union and keeping the institution of slavery became more apparent, the Mendenhall family, who deeply disapproved of slavery, finally came to the decision that, like so many Quakers in that region, they should promptly emigrate to Ohio or Indiana in the North. To do this meant abandoning the New Garden Friends Boarding School. But the die was cast and the family, with all of their transportable belongings, were at the train station in Greensboro ready to leave.

With the many complications that might come from the reopening of the decision to leave that had been so burningly clear to them up to this time, the Inward Guide laid firmly on Nerius Mendenhall that he must not leave; that he must return to the school; and that, come what would, he must bear his witness right there where he had been placed. He shared this call with his wife and she concurred. They carted their belongings and their family back to their home and settled in. He kept the school open all during the Civil War and took a leading role in the Reconstruction that followed these horrible years. Today, New Garden Friends Boarding School is Guilford College, one of the most promising of the smaller colleges in the South.

Emma Noble was the wife of a foreman in a locomotive works near Oxford in Britain. In the early 1920s, the unemployment and misery in the coal mining areas of South Wales were appalling. It came to her in a Quaker meeting for worship that she would visit this area and see if there was anything that the Quakers could do to lessen the pain. Her husband agreed, and a small committee of clearness in the Meeting found the concern in the right ordering and encouraged her to follow it. In the first valley that she visited in South Wales, there seemed to be no opening for the kind of assistance that the Friends could offer. She did not feel released to return home, however, and extending her journey, she looked into the Rhondda Valley. In the course of some days there, a way began to open and the real purpose of her journey began to emerge. Out of the visit, a way was found to release the Nobles for what turned out to be some years of service, and a longtime program of work unfolded that eventually involved university people, members of parliament, a royal visit, and finally a program of legislation to help to ease the ugly situation. Her first small step, which was in part a mistaken one, led to further steps and ultimately to a deeper and deeper involvement.

These examples give at least a glimpse of the manner in which concerns arise and are carried through, with failures and unpredictable breakthroughs all mixed in. Malty Babcock, a British religious leader in the last generation, used to say that Jesus promised those who would follow his leadings only three things: that they should be absurdly happy, entirely fearless, and always in trouble! Most concerns begin as seeds that may need scarifying in order to grow. Not only is the seed of concern something that needs careful treatment to unfold, but the one to whom the concern has come may often be quite unready to carry it out until he or she has been changed and reshaped in ways that call for great flexibility and openness. Even the community that is to encourage and support the concern may have to go through painful change before it is ready to unite with the concern.

These leadings of the Guide come to us by the route of our own psychological mechanisms and are capable therefore of blemish. A seasoned Friend has a certain debonair attitude about being made a fool of and has learned how to wait and see how the concern and the motives for that concern look the next day or the next week. One knows enough to allow one's own private detective agency to examine all aspects of one's concern. A Friend sees how it looks after wise and trusted people who have been consulted have given their opinions of it. If the concern can endure this kind of scrutiny, one may take it to a committee of clearness that one may select oneself. If it involves the Meeting, the individual may ask to bring it to a monthly meeting for business. The "when in doubt, wait" motto, painful as it may seem to the person or persons involved, has been found so often to test the flexibility and really centered spirit of the bearer of the concern. If this embarrassing waiting, or the prospect of it, succeeds in dissolving away the concern, the concern's rootlessness has been exposed and it withers away and can be buried. Albert Schweitzer once suggested that when some compassionate venture, perhaps of an innovative sort, is proposed, we must not expect people to clear stones from our path. Rather, they may roll a few extra boulders onto the path just to see if we really mean it!

My own life as a professor of philosophy has, from the time I was thirty-six years of age, been sprinkled with interwoven concerns for situations in the world, and through Haverford College's academic generosity, I have been able to travel in Europe, and later with my wife in Africa and Asia, on many missions for the American Friends Service Committee (AFSC) and the Friends World Committee. I have known the delay, the blocking, the yielding, and often the concern turning out so very differently from what I had originally conceived it to be. I have also experienced breakthroughs that went beyond my fondest hopes. I had been in Finland in 1937 and was deeply drawn to these fascinating people. The frightful winter war with Russia in 1939-40 had taken a terrible toll, and when I was called upon by the AFSC to spend some months in Germany in the last half of 1940, I felt a strong leading to visit Finland and to see if anything could be done to ease their sense of despair and of being totally abandoned. Over the months, in spite of vigorous efforts to help me from what remained of the Christian underground at that time, I was repeatedly refused the necessary visas that were required in wartime to leave and reenter Germany. Finally, at the end of November when my time in Germany was almost up, I was informed by the ministry that had assisted me in these requests that the final denial, the *Nicht Gestattet,* had come from the Gestapo at Alexanderplatz and that the matter was closed.

This concern of mine had been from the depths, and I went back quite shaken to the little Berlin Quaker Center and settled in the meetinghouse room for a time of quiet. It seemed correct in the course of the silent waiting that I go to Dr. Diekoff, the German ambassador to the United States, who sat in Berlin during the war period, to describe my situation, and then that I should lay aside this concern, for all its gripping character, and give myself fully to another round of visits to the German Quakers before leaving for America at the end of the year.

I set out the next day for this round of visits and, three days later, when I was visiting a brave Christian pastor near Bückeburg who was very close to the Society of Friends, I was called back to Berlin by my colleague there, who had just been notified by the Gestapo that my exit and reentry visas were waiting for me at Alexanderplatz. I was able with his help to fly to Sweden the next evening and to make the Finnish visit, a visit that in many ways led to the Quaker relief work for the north of Finland that I was to organize five years later. An International Folk-Highschool called Viittakivi also grew out of the relief work and the work camps that we carried on so closely with the Finnish Christian Settlement

Movement. This experience of being willing to accept the refusal of my journey to Finland, followed by its restoration, seemed almost as if I had to learn the meaning of seventeenth-century spiritual guide Bérulle's searching counsel, "To go or to stay is the same." Only as I was willing to give it up and to "stay" was the way open for me to go forward.

I will mention only one other situation as a personal example of a concern that failed completely and yet emerged some years later in a dramatically different form that, in the end, actually carried out the original leading in an amazing fashion. In 1960 on a mission for the AFSC in India, my wife and I were much drawn to confer and to search for a suitable place for a possible modest Quaker ashram, with Gurdial Malik, an Indian Quaker of deep spiritual gifts, as a warden and presence. We thought of it as an ecumenical center of hospitality where, from time to time, spiritual personalities from the Christian and other great world religions would be invited to live together and irradiate each other with the rich experiences of their different traditions. The search utterly failed.

In 1966, six years later, my earlier leading for this deep exposure to each other of Christians and Hindus in India and Christians and Zen Buddhists in Japan surfaced again. With the approval of the Friends World Committee and a year of careful preparation (where I was admirably assisted by several Roman Catholic presences whom I had known at Vatican Council II in Rome), two residential colloquiums, one of five days and the other of seven, were able to be held in 1967, one in Japan and one in India. Each colloquium was made up of ten carefully chosen Christian men of the spirit who in Japan were matched by ten Zen Buddhist masters and in India by ten outstanding Hindu Sadhus and scholars. In each case all were the guests of the Quakers. The meetings, however, were not held on Quaker soil or under a Quaker roof, for which I had been searching fruitlessly in 1960, but in most suitable conference centers in each country!

Late in August 1986 this Japanese colloquium held its twentieth annual meeting for some three days in Kyōto, alternating every other year with a meeting in Tokyo. A moving book appeared in 1977 called *A Zen-Christian Pilgrimage*, with twenty-six personal chapters describing what this experience of meeting annually with those of another religion, for a whole decade, had meant to each individual's own religious life. Four years later the English translation of the book was printed. Gurdial Malik is no longer alive, and there is still no physically established Quaker ashram in either country! Yet in this situation, as in the unforeseen unfolding of so many concerns, the waiting, the drastic reshaping, or even the deferment to a future generation does not invalidate its significance.

On a bulletin board in the little Quaker meetinghouse in Australia's Adelaide, I once saw some words from a British Quaker educator, the late Harold Loucks, that read, "An act of love that fails is just as much a part of the divine life as an act of love that succeeds. For love is measured by its fullness and not by its reception." To do what we are led to do by concern and to leave the rest with the Master Harvester seems to Quakers to be the way indicated.

When, late in his life, John Woolman felt drawn to make the dangerous trip to Wehaloosing in order to visit the friendly tribe of Indians who had called on the Quakers in Philadelphia, he wrote in his *Journal*, "Love was the first motion." I have been witnessing to my faith and experience that love *is* the first motion, a love that will not let us go, yet a love that lures us to respond and to follow the biddings of the Inward Guide.

To understand the Christian religion with all of its widely varying forms of worship and expression—its mystical, its prophetic, its mutual caring outreach to the world's needs—one must return to the divine love at the heart of things that undergirds us all and, above all, one must realize that we are not in this alone.

Arthur Gossip, a hard-bitten pastor in a slum church in Glasgow, tells of how, at the end of a long day of visiting his parishioners, he arrived late in the afternoon at a five-story tenement where the last family on his list for that day lived at the very top. He was done in and said to himself, "It's too far up. I'll come tomorrow." He was about to turn away when a pair of stooped gray shoulders seemed to brush past him and start up the stairs with the word, "Then I'll have to go alone." Arthur Gossip added, "We went together."

NOTES

1. E. Underhill, *Practical Mysticism* (New York: E. P. Dutton, 1915), 11.
2. E. Underhill, *Mysticism* (London: Methuen, 1911), 532.
3. *Meister Eckhart*, ed. Franz Pfeiffer, trans. C de B. Evans (London: John M. Watkins, 1924), 231.
4. *St. Bernard on Song of Songs* (London: Mowbry, 1952).
5. Alexander Parker, *Letters of Friends*, ed. A. R. Barclay, 1841, 365-66.
6. Donald Court, "On Coping with Our Double Life," *The Friend*, 128, (1970), 1109.
7. Anthony Bloom, *Beginning to Pray* (New York: Paulist), 59-61.
8. William James, *The Varieties of Religious Experience* (New York: Longmans), 388.
9. Adrienne von Speyr, *The Word*, trans. Alexander Dru (London: Collins, 1955), 109.

2.

ON THE POWER OF SUSTAINED ATTENTION

"On the Power of Sustained Attention" was my response to an invitation from Agnes Scott College in Georgia in the 1950s to give the annual Phi Beta Kappa Lecture. It was first printed in 1960 in a Festshrift volume, Then and Now, *honoring Henry J. Cadbury, Harvard's distinguished New Testament scholar, who was a Quaker and a dear friend whom I greatly admired. The text has been revised in some instances in order to make its language more inclusive.*

If I were pressed to name the most neglected factor in higher education today, I think I would name the power of sustained attention. This neglect may stem from its being so completely taken for granted at every stage of education that it can simply be assumed to be present and the matter can therefore be dismissed. The late Principal L. P. Jacks used to tell of a parlor game in his home where each guest was given a limited time in which to list all that he saw in a room. He noted that almost no guest ever listed the light by which the objects were able to be seen at all.

If this quality of sustained attention can be lifted out into the center for examination, it may turn out to be the very hallmark of a truly educated person. It could certainly be argued that the rest of formal education is only the material which such a power of sustained attention is capable of ordering. In a few years following the period of formal education most of these materials will slip away, for memory unbinds as well as binds. But people who have developed the power of exposing themselves with utter humility and utter abandon before a field or a person or a problem can draw the relevant materials into focus again, and have about them the authentic mark of educated people.

This power of attention which we possess is an amazing gift. Philosophers, quite rightly, seized upon it as a compelling piece of evidence for being free and not determined. We can listen or we can relax our attention or direct it elsewhere.

We can drowse or we can draw a bead and engage with all that is being said. The Germans have a word to describe the kind of relaxation of attention that often takes place in Sunday pews. They call it *Kirchenschlaf*. It does not differ greatly from what might be termed *Akademikerschlaf*. A speaker in a church or in a college classroom usually gets more, not less, attention than is deserved, and Phillips Brooks was certainly no more than reasonable when he told his verger that if he saw anyone sleeping during his sermons he was to come at once to the pulpit and wake the preacher up. But this power we possess of turning on or withholding the spotlight of attention from that which confronts us is a gift so close to the core of what makes us persons that other powers fade before it; and in each exercise of it there is something self-confirming about our status as free and responsible persons.

THE LURE OF THIS POWER OF SUSTAINED ATTENTION

When we see this gift of concentrated attention operating superbly in others, we are overcome with a longing to possess more of it ourselves. A schoolgirl came to her father one day in high spring as he was working in his garden. She told him that she had just come from the meadow where she had gone after school and had been lying on her back there listening to hear every sound that could be heard, looking about quietly to see every sight that could be seen, and smelling to sense every smell that could be smelled. Who can hear of such youthful adventures in attentive awareness without a yearning to share them, to waken out of the numb, stuporous drowse, and to become aware, awake, ablaze with attentive openness?

In the years after the First World War, Salvador de Madariaga y Rojo, already a Spanish statesman and man of letters, was carrying heavy responsibility at the League of Nations. He was secretary of the Disarmament Commission and held half a dozen other portfolios, as most of the gifted men did in this young and expanding world forum. Several of his colleagues were talking of the staggering loads of work they were saddled with, and complaining of how they could get only five or six hours of sleep at night because they were so pressed. They turned to Madariaga, who carried more than any of them, and asked him how long he slept each night. He replied that he always slept nine hours. They pitched upon him and asked how he could possibly do what he did and still get so long a rest. He laughed and said, "But see how much more awake I am now than you are!"

Certain schools of Japanese art which are contemptuous of photographic reproduction in painting and bent upon catching the inward meaning of nature and depicting it on their scrolls have a highly suggestive discipline for their novice painters. When pupils are painting a mountain, before they set down a line on the paper, they must sit before the mountain, direct toward it their most complete attention, feel into it; and only after hours of such attention undertake to sketch and paint it. "I look at the mountain," one of them writes, "until I have an inner image which is made up of all that I have been able to comprehend of what it means within itself. Then I paint my experience of the mountain."

A sculptor who used to teach and work in his shop at Olivet College was describing to a friend of mine how he worked. He said that he developed in his mind the figure he wanted to produce and then, without any clay or plaster of paris intermediaries, he just chopped away the stone between him and his concentrated vision until it stood embodied in the rock there before him.

Any of you who have read Tolstoy's great novel *Resurrection* know how Nekhlúdoff seemed to have a power of concentrated attention which enabled him to see in the prostitute prisoner Katusha a woman of noble being, worthy of faith and honor and sacrifice, and that the persistence of this vision finally awakened it in Katusha herself and set her free. The New Testament records instance after instance of this power of attention in far greater measure in Jesus. The miserable taxgatherer, Zacchaeus, who was looked upon as a local quisling, grown wealthy at the expense of others and beneath their contempt, sat perched on the limb of the tree when Jesus passed. Jesus seemed to see in this man something none of the townspeople saw, a new man waiting to be born, and the account says that he called out to him to come down and be his host for the day. This power of attention seems to give to those who possess it new eyes for invisibles.

Some years ago, I spent eleven days in French Equatorial Africa at the jungle hospital of Albert Schweitzer near Lambaréné, and I saw this man at all hours of the day and night carrying on his work. Whether he was organizing a crew of reluctant Africans to unload a boat of lumber, or guiding the laying of a cement foundation and floor for a fruit cellar, or inspecting the building of an addition to the simple quarters for nurses and guests; whether he was greeting a guest and personally showing him to his room and to the facilities, or practicing on his steel piano, or writing letters, or working on his book deep into the night, or on his knees utterly absorbed in watching a ten-minute-old antelope try to rally its long pipe-stem legs to make its first erect stand in this world, or showing a visitor the mysteries of the Southern cross in the starry equatorial heavens, or talking to a fifteen-year-old dog at the dining room door and asking him which of them he thought would outlive the other, Doctor Schweitzer seemed to be giving to each task his entire, complete, and undivided attention. He seemed to live for nothing except that moment, and to be utterly and completely open to the needs of that moment, and to receive the full impact of the impressions of that moment. *The Cloud of Unknowing* has fascinated its readers for almost six centuries by describing the complete joy of contemplative prayer where the worshiper is totally engaged in doing something now that one would gladly go on doing forever!

These examples may indicate something of what I mean by attention, by the capacity to turn the light upon what is before us and to be teachable before it, that is, to be open to receive what it has to teach us, or to put our queries to it, or confront it with our hypotheses and divinations and then dare to receive its honest answers. The person who has the capacity to direct attention in this way and to sustain it is an educated person. And the one who has no such capacity cannot replace the lack by any of the taken-on decorations of learning.

Now my presupposition in this exalting of the power of sustained attention is that men and women are meant to be open to reality, that reality in its many dimensions is continuously communicating itself to us; and that "'tis ye, 'tis your estranged faces, that miss the many-splendoured thing." It presupposes that the real is there, that it is given, that we do not make it but that when we attend to it with a clear, teachable openness, whether in another person, in nature, in a problem in chemistry or in mathematics, or in confronting the ultimate frame, or the deity in which all of these are gathered up, we shall be able to encounter, to engage with, and to register the impact and the meaning of this vital episode.

CAN THE POWER OF SUSTAINED ATTENTION BE CULTIVATED?

The problem then emerges: Can this power of attention be cultivated, or is attention like the psychologist's early view of the IQ, a fixed dispensation? Is trying to develop the capacity for attention as hopeless as watering a broomstick in the hope that it will one day sprout and grow or as tapping a telegraph pole in the hope of starting a run of maple sap? Given a reasonably normal person to begin with, the weight of evidence supports the position that the power of sustained attention can be rewardingly cultivated, and this would seem to strengthen the conviction that it is the very heart of the task of true education to assist that process.

But after this has been said, it must be admitted that power of attention is the name for a condition of intellectual and spiritual health which is the convergence of many factors. The approach to it may be delicate and may require as much oblique movement and stealth as to overtake and observe the nature of pleasure without causing it to vanish. One of my professors at Harvard used to define pleasure as a physical by-product, and to refer to it as "the hum of the motor when it is hitting on all six." Is it conceivable that attention is the culmination of a certain inward ordering of many factors so that when this ordering is present, one is able to concentrate, to attend; and when this order is absent, the power of attention, if it remains at all, is sporadic, dispersed, and blurred? There may be some confirmation of this hypothesis in the fact that when a person becomes nervously distraught, the two ways in which it shows first are almost invariably in a disturbance of rest with resulting insomnia, and in a disturbance of the capacity for sustained attention with resulting destruction of the power to concentrate.

If we go more carefully into the matter, we find that there is, in the ordering process that releases attention, a set of what might be called supporting centers of interest and information, which it is one of education's chief functions to provide. In that initial warming-up process, which seems to be quite as essential for attention as for a radio tube, past knowledge and objects of previous attention assist greatly.

If I am a bird expert, I am keyed up to hear bird calls which another may miss entirely. A little twelve-year-old girl who plays the slide trombone tugged at her mother's arm when a piece of instrumental music was played at a theater and whispered, "Listen to that trombone, Mother." A historian brightens at the mention of the Treaty of Vienna, and a student of Renaissance literature quickens when he discovers that Donne wrote the sonnet on the Resurrection which uses the language of alchemy and refers to the risen Jesus as a tincture that could change base metals into gold. These things we lay down piece by piece without being conscious that we are drawing upon them. They are of great assistance in the initial focus of attention. They seem to lower the threshold over which attention may stream in. These centers of interest and information cross-fertilize each other and they are indefinitely expandable. It is another case of "to him that hath shall be given and from him that hath not shall be taken away even that which he hath."

Something takes place, however, that is more than a cross-fertilization of these centers of interest and information which makes one field light up another. There seems to be an actual transfer of training between the ability to attend intensively in one field and the same ability in another field. If I learn to concentrate in learning the French or Latin language, I seem to be able to use this same gift not only with other languages but in overcoming the resistance to attention in a problem in economics or a tough stretch of history as well. Simone Weil in her remarkable essay *Waiting for God* goes so far as to suggest that effective concentration on Latin, which was so difficult for the peasant student of theology who later became the Curé d'Ars and was canonized in 1925, paid off in assisting his capacity to attend without strain to the problems of the thousands who came to him from all stations of life and from all over France to make their confessions and to secure his amazingly searching spiritual counsel. Simone Weil implies as well that to learn to concentrate on a rugged geometry problem which results in seeing how the parts of space fit coherently together will help prepare a mind for the most difficult and most needed concentration of all, that which is called meditation and prayer.

VOLUNTARY AND INVOLUNTARY PROCESSES IN ATTENTION

It would be misleading in speaking about this power of attention and our freedom to direct it where we will if I gave the impression that we are attentive when we wrench our consciousness around to a certain area and, by tightly clenching our fists and head muscles, try to force our attention to remain there. This kind of violence of the will in the matter of attention is possible to us, and I do not mean to underestimate its place in our human equipment. Most of us, however, know all too well what it is to force ourselves to face a book on biology or history and to turn the pages one after another, coming up at the end of an hour with almost no intake whatever. But this muscle knotting is not to be confused with attention, although I will not deny that in the period before we are warmed up, some firm acts of will or the habit of past acts of will may be necessary to expose us to the work that is before us. Ignoring this is the original fallacy of progressive education. Any writer knows the initial agony of getting to one's desk at a given hour, the victim of a hundred distractions, until one screws oneself down, goes over yesterday's writing, or begins to set something down and gets warmed up. Then attention really flows out until the writer forgets time and place and becomes inwardly absorbed in what that writer is about.

In the life of prayer and meditation, the situation is almost identical. Without an act of will or habit to get us past this initial dispersion and lethargy, nothing happens. Once past it, with attention in full play, we go beyond ourselves into that interplay of spirit which slowly moves our deepest centers of interest over into a sympathetic response to that which we confront.

There would seem to be revealed here an indication that there is an initial level of voluntary, that is, self-directed and self-willed, attention to guide and direct on which some pressure of the will is necessary, and then, depending greatly upon processes which have become second nature, that is skills and experience, a level of involuntary or effortless or object-guided attention takes over. It is here that the deepest things are communicated to us and it is here that the best work is done. Unless this second level of involuntary attention enters in, the first thrust of voluntary, will-powered attention is likely to fade swiftly and our minds are likely quickly to slither off into other fields.

THE ROLE OF DESIRE AND CONCERN IN ATTENTION

Of even deeper importance than the second-nature processes of interest and information, although in no sense conflicting with them or diminishing their importance, is the person's desire or hunger or longing to move into this field that is before one. The tame, smug, sluggish, torpid, complacent, domesticated minds of so many of our over-privileged Western youth will never have more than a shallow and surface interest in what is offered in a liberal arts education today. They are not hungry. They have made no considerable personal sacrifice to get to a university. There is for them no burning urgency. They are not asking the questions to which some answers might be given in what they are confronting. I have talked with Polish students who risked their lives in the years 1939-45, when the German conquerors had forbidden all higher education in Poland, in order to go secretly to tutors to learn. I know that in Polish internment camps in Germany people stayed up half the night to recite poetry to each other, to teach each other their skills, when they knew they had to face, on a ration of scant bread and soup, twelve hours of forced labor that would begin before daybreak the next day. Albert Schweitzer told me of a little band of students, of which he was a member, at the University of Strasbourg who learned Hebrew in a class of their own from 11 P.M. to 1 A.M. each night because they needed the language to read the Old Testament in the original!

I can recall the way my Haverford colleague, Thomas Kelly, after a transforming inward experience which he went through in the winter of 1937-38, began to read writings of the mystics—Teresa of Avila, John of the Cross, Fox, and Woolman—in order to try to find out if they knew about and could help him to assimilate the light that had come to him. A mother searching a Red Cross handbook to find out how to fasten a tourniquet on her child's bleeding arm could not have read more avidly than did Thomas Kelly that winter.

All of us attend most naturally to what we long to know. The words "where your heart is, there will your treasure be also" might well be amplified as an English schoolmistress once explained them for Janet Payne Whitney, saying that you find where your treasure is by noting what it is that your mind turns to without effort when it is left to its own movement.

THE PASCALIAN CLEFT

Most of us, however, are not sure that we want to know the truth with the avidity and abandon with which these seekers wanted it. And that to which our minds turn without effort is neither what we allege we want nor what we honestly believe would permanently satisfy us if we had it. We find our minds divided, especially in matters that have a bearing on our own style of life.

Somewhat wistfully and enviously we read Augustine's words in *Confessions:* "I was collected from the dispersion in which I turned from Thee, the One, and was vainly divided." Pascal, however, describes our unredeemed, uncollected, dispersed experience more accurately when he speaks in *Thoughts* about how "in every man there is an infinite abyss that can only be filled by an infinite and immutable Object." This cleft or abyss is all too well-known to us.

A woman who had organized many Berea College extension or opportunity schools in the Kentucky mountains once told me how on one occasion she brought to Berea College itself a group of her mountaineer friends to be guests of the college for a week. She had arranged a program of college lectures for them. In the course of one of the lectures, a Berea College professor had spoken to them of the race question in a way that was far too revolutionary for their way of thinking about blacks. At the end of the lecture these mountaineers said nothing to the professor and got up to leave, but my friend, who recognized their smoldering hostility to what had been said, asked them to sit down again and to tell the professor exactly what they felt and talk it out with him. This they proceeded to do in no uncertain terms. One of the men, however, did not come back but stood in a corner, and my friend went over to talk with him. She asked him why he had not joined the others in the discussion. He replied that he didn't care to. She asked him if he was satisfied with what the professor had said, and he shook his head. She pressed him further until he said, "I'll tell you, mum, with my head I could see sense in all he said, but down here," and he ran his hand from his neck to his waist, "I was against every word of it. And until I can get myself together, mum, I'm going to keep my mouth shut."

FORCES IN US THAT BLOCK ATTENTION

This abyss, this dispersion, this division between what makes sense to the mind but has all our emotional and visceral patterns behind our reluctance to follow it is familiar ground, and it does not take a magnetic detector to disclose the forces in us that deflect the compass from true magnetic north and keep the needle of attention in a constant state of agitation.

Some of us dare not have our old frames of thought disturbed. At an early age we have become afflicted with what could be called "hardening of the categories," a disease that has constricted the whole world's vision today so that we can no longer attend to persons and situations or see them as they really are. If I classify persons or nations as thieves, I expect them always to fulfill that role and I can no longer pay attention to their actions objectively.

In Nova Scotia where I once spent a summer, I was told

when I arrived that a neighbor was a thief. One morning when I was down in my little studyhouse near the sea, I heard the boat chain rattle and heard the boat being scraped over the stones as it was being launched. I looked out and saw this neighbor about to push off in my boat. I called out to him and asked why he was taking my boat, to which he replied that my wife had given him permission, which indeed she had! Our frames of rigidly fixed expectations often deflect attention, and prevent our seeing what is there. They go even further. They may even lead us to see what is not there.

Often self-interest twists attention or spirits it away lest it expose us. We may not be as obvious about it as the two young men who were sitting in a crowded street car. One is said to have noticed that his friend had his eyes closed and asked him why he did not open them, to which the other replied that he just could not bear to see women standing! Even Darwin knew that he must make a special effort to note and instantly record evidence that tended to disprove his theories because if he put it off, he was likely to ignore or forget it. According to Albert Day, a scientist once made a fortnight's investigation on the spot of the evidence behind the psychological work in extrasensory perception which Professor Rhine in those days had done at Duke University. The scientist went away unconvinced although he admitted that after a full examination he could find no flaw whatever in the methods used or the calculations from the data obtained. To admit Rhine's data as legitimate would have compelled him to change his whole frame of reference, and he was not prepared for this.

In the New Testament there is a story of events in the Gadarene district where there is no doubt whatever about the miraculous powers of Jesus to heal the mentally distressed. But the inhabitants of the region asked him to take those powers away and not to return with them because in the course of his healing a maniac, the community lost too many swine. There are more than a few of us who cannot attend to what is before us with a full and clear and teachable mind because unconsciously at least we sense all too clearly what the conclusions we would reach might cost us, what swine might have to go. Many of us want the power of sustained attention, but we do not want what brings it about. *The Imitation of*

Christ says, "All desire peace, but they do not desire the things that lead to true peace," or again, "All desire to contemplate, but they do not desire what leads to true contemplation."

Instead of that position of humility which is the only security that will enable us to attend in a profound way to the truth before us, we keep attending desperately to all the inward and outward voices at once in the hope of hearing one that will be more to our advantage. Years ago I knew an old college president, Raymond Binford, who was somewhat deaf. He had called one of his students to his office in order to ask him how much he would charge him to do a piece of work in clearing up his front yard, and went on signing his letters as the student stood before him. "How much would you charge me?" he asked. The student said, "About two dollars." He went on signing letters and a few minutes later he asked again, "How much would you charge me for that job?" The student had thought it over in the meantime and felt that he had asked too little, so he said, "Oh, about two dollars and a half." The President straightened up and said, "Algie, I heard thee the first time."

NOT SCIENCE BUT SCIENTISM CONTRACTS THE SPAN OF ATTENTION

The kind of selective listening that leaves out what it does not want to hear is not unknown to the parents of keen children. And strangely enough, it is the hallmark of what was once a highly popular brand of philosophy in England and America which was known as logical positivism or what I would prefer to call Scientism. This school of thought has sought to cloak itself with the authority of science and to rule out of the orbit of attention anything except the processes of scientific discovery and communication. The result is the production of a kind of cataract growth over the focus of attention that either directly or by a conspiracy of silence excludes the great issues of life that call for a heroic response.

For centuries science has been rightly indulged in its abbreviations when it ignores whole sections of reality—the moral, the aesthetic, the spiritual—and confines its attention to the processes of the physical world or more recently to an attempt to study the processes at work in the social and political and psychological realms. This indulgence has been not only proper but highly rewarding. But when this abbreviation, this dropping out of one's central concerns in life, is not acknowledged as a temporary utilitarian expedient, and when the very fact that it is an abbreviation is forgotten, and the processes of discovery and communication within this limited segment of reality are alleged, as they were by the logical positivists, to be all that there is, we get the shrinkage of the field of attention and of vision with which this shallow scientism, blown up into a philosophy, has afflicted us.

WHERE SCIENTISM FAILS US

The crisis brought on by the threat of cosmic disaster has with an incredible swiftness removed this intellectual cataract. It has thrown light upon the utter poverty of this scientism and its worship, and has begun to disclose to us in our desperation the necessity of reopening the range of our attention. From many sides the evidence pours in. A Swedish trade union leader has learned the hard way that out of the science of union tactics alone, you do not get a principle strong enough to hold the rich unions in line and make them open their well-stocked treasuries to the poor, unorganized timber and agricultural workers in an effort to lift up their level of life.

In Hiroshima after the bomb fell, writer John Hersey tells us in his documentary novel of that scene, as the crowds rushed through the ember-strewn streets heading for the suburbs to escape the burning inferno, trapped victims, caught under timbers in the burning houses, screamed for someone to come and release them. Most of the panic-ridden refugees did not even hear the cries of these victims, so absorbed were they in their own misery. Some, however, dimly heard them and reasoned that this was the job for the air raid relief teams, the police, the soldiery; or they eased their minds by telling themselves that even if they did go in they might not save them anyhow. So they hurried on their way. Here and there someone heard the cries, attended to them, saw what was required, dropped out of line, went to the rescue, released the trapped victims, and staggered on with them. In our terrible need today, Scientism disclaims all responsibility either for laying responsibility for one people upon those with whom they are at variance or for drawing out of people this third type of response to need and damping down the other two. If pressed, it has little to offer outside of proposing another new bureau of propaganda, this time presumably for the promotion of mutual aid.

When in the early days after Pearl Harbor the governor of Colorado put his political future at stake by refusing to include his state in the hysterical move to prevent Japanese from moving in and settling there, he stopped an avalanche far up the mountain where it had little force. When no rent control laws could touch a group of tough French mountain peasants and compel them to take into their spacious homes some miserable homeless families living in terrible squalor on the edge of town, a winter of evening sessions on a section of the New Testament compelled their leader to declare that they must either lay that book down and open it no more or else open their homes—which a number of them did. To open the orbit of attention to the total frame and to what it demands of us is, to put it mildly, dangerous but indispensable business.

EDUCATION AND OUR VITAL AXIOMS

Because of the threat to ourselves which is involved in attention, it is unlikely that the screen of attention will be left free to record in deep humility what is there, or to shift the focus from the surface features of what is present to the deeper meaning of that encounter and what it demands of us. We must be willing to die to what is false or trivial, no matter what the cost. But no psyche ever seeks such painful sacrifice or is prepared for such an inward purging of disorder unless it does so in order to respond to something which it deeply desires.

T. E. Hulme, in *Speculations*, speaks of the vital axioms deep within each of us which do not necessarily express our much-talked-of ideals, but which are the canons of satisfaction by which we make our choices. If you make a graph of your choices you may know more about the vital axioms which really guide your action than if you take part in a surface discussion of your life preferences while your desire for social approval is looking over your shoulder. Now these vital axioms are not fixed. They are subject to change, and wherever education is really about its full task, it freely acknowledges that it is concerned that such a change should take place. But it can change the axioms only by making us want to attend to the highest to which we are capable of responding.

If the remark of Leon Bloy's character at the close of his novel *The Woman Who Was Poor* has any meaning for us, it might arouse in us a want that we have scarcely dared to acknowledge. *"There is only one unhappiness,"* the character says, *"and that is—NOT TO BE ONE OF THE SAINTS."* Saints for him are ordinary people who are inwardly attending to the highest truth they know and who are prepared to let this truth have more and more undivided sway in their lives. The saints are not afraid of consequences because they are such avid lovers of the truth they have found. It is blasphemy to talk in the presence of saints about the sacrifices they make. David Livingstone, who had lost his beloved wife with fever and had undergone untold hardships in his travels in the heart of Africa, insisted that "in all my life I never made a sacrifice." He had simply done what he most deeply wanted to do. Matilda Wrede, the great Finnish woman apostle to the prisoners of her country, who spent her life on these men and women, many of whom deceived her, lied to her, cheated her, and failed her again and again, said when, worn out, she lay dying, "Has anyone in this generation had such a joyous life as mine?" She had done what she most truly wanted to do. Simone Weil, the French-Jewish heroine martyr of the Free French resistance movement whose spiritual writings have so deeply moved postwar France, would have scoffed at talk of her sacrifices. Although she died in London in 1943 at the age of thirty-four of a malady that was aggravated by her refusal to eat more than the official factory ration of her factory-worker friends inside France itself, she worked and wrote and did to the very end what she most wanted to do.

AS ATTENTIVE "AS YOU WISH TO BE"

The deep hunger and positive motivation required to produce sustained attention depend upon what we really want most. Some young priests came to the great mystic Jan van Ruysbroeck at Groenendael just outside of Brussels late in his life and asked him how they could order their lives so as to become holy men. His reply was brief and abrupt. He said, "You are as holy as you wish to be!" In the matter of attention it can be as simply said. It is our desire, our longing, our willingness to put all aside in order to possess this gift and what it will confront us with that is the principal condition of obtaining it.

I am not suggesting that education is or should be primarily designed to make saints and martyrs. But it would take a short memory to forget the moral abdication of the continental university-trained intellectuals which furnished the setting for Romain Rolland's prophetic statement in his book *I Will Not Rest* where he declares, "But among those who clamor for independence of thought, how many have this faith and above all the sincere desire to realize it? How many are really the servants of truth, loyal, disinterested and determined to go to the very end of truth? I have not failed to know, I have known it since my youth (I have denounced it through the voice of my Jean Christophe) that the intellectuals, the great majority of them, were unfaithful to their duty, unequal to their task, and the independence they professed was conditioned by their real servility to the masters of public opinion, the dispensers of honors and of benefits." What I am implying here is that unless a liberal education can confront men and women with great principles of life and can draw them to attend to this truth in such a sustained way that its implications become compelling for their own lives, then this form of education will be brushed aside and will give way to a technical specialization that will crowd in to replace it.

I freely admit that what I have said here about the cultivation of the gift of sustained attention is little more than a rudimentary framework for a philosophy of contemplation. This is no accidental coincidence, however, for it is only when education dares to help provide such a rudimentary framework for our highest activity that the principles of order for its higher ranges are ever adequately provided. And until in every generation there are men and women who are educated so as to dare to look into the heart of the universe and attend to it and order their lives in keeping with what they find there, our world will be poor and ragged and bound hand and foot by fear.

Dogged as men and women are today by the threat of cosmic arson, there is a sense in which our world in both East and West seems to be moving in a profound somnambulism, climbing along window ledges and crossing parapets that are so dangerous that we dare not awaken lest we stagger and pitch headlong into the abyss. It is in such a time that we need men and women with so great a power of sustained attention that each might take as his or her point of intent to seek "to walk through the dream of life as one awake."

3.

Evelyn Underhill and the Mid-Life Transformation

"Evelyn Underhill's Mid-Life Transformation" has never before appeared in print. It was a part of the first of a series of five lectures that I gave in the summer of 1978 in the annual Douglas Steere Lecture series under the Methodists' Bay View Association, which has conducted religious services there for well over a century.

In this brief chapter I want to share with you a glimpse of a remarkable British woman of our own century who wrote under her maiden name, Evelyn Underhill, although she was not a feminist and was happily married to Hubert Stuart Moore in 1907. She was already in her thirties when she married. By that time she had begun to have a following as a writer, and she never bothered to change her pen name. Much has been said in our time about the mid-life crisis in both women and men with subsequent tragedies or creative breakthroughs. In the dimension of the spiritual life, I cannot think of a more fascinating window to this mid-life crisis than is to be found in the life of Evelyn Underhill. Marriage, career, success, despondency, the wise counsel of an almost matchless spiritual guide, a breakthrough followed by a dozen wonderful years of books, letters, and spiritual counseling are all to be found and to be feasted on in a look at her adult life.

I have especially cherished the books of this latter period in her life, for she was perhaps the most able intellectual follower of Baron Friedrich von Hügel. He was an astonishing German Roman Catholic scholar and interpreter of the interior life, who lived his adult life in Britain and was regarded as the ablest Christian mind in that country during the first quarter of this century. Von Hügel, with all of his array of languages, his immense reading and grasp of the modern situation in religious affairs, and the fact that he wrote nearly all of his books in English, admitted that he did at least 60 percent of his thinking in German. He had a style of writing that, as George Tyrrell suggested, was suitable only for arch-angels in retreat to read and to understand.

In Evelyn Underhill, on the other hand, we have not only a first-class mind but a poet and writer with wit and style and clarity, who has used the best insights of von Hügel's Existential Realism as the frame in which she has interpreted prayer and worship. We have, therefore, not only devotional writing but writing that is framed by a philosophical and theological map that can bear the sharpest scrutiny. A previous Archbishop of Canterbury, Michael Ramsey, in speaking about Evelyn Underhill and her influence on what we would call the Episcopal Church, noted, "There are few, if indeed any, in the Church of England who did more to help people to grasp the priority of prayer in the Christian life and the place of the contemplative element in it." And with this, we might have a look first at her life and then at several facets of her counsel on the nurture of the interior life.

I find it very easy to remember the dates of Evelyn Underhill's birth and death for she was born in 1875, the same year as my own mother, and she died in 1941, just a year after my mother's death. In the autumn of 1927, I was working at Oxford in collecting material for an eventual doctoral thesis at Harvard on Baron Friedrich von Hügel. Someone had written to Evelyn Underhill telling her of my interest in von Hügel. I will insert here a little piece from my own memoirs that cover that period.

At her invitation I went one afternoon to have tea with Evelyn Underhill (Mrs. Stuart Moore), whose very life has been shaped by von Hügel in the last three years before his death and who, in the decade before her own death in 1941, became one of the baron's most impressive interpreters. I was prepared to enjoy the visit with her, for I had heard that, like the attractive fourteenth-century anchoress, Mother Julian of Norwich, she was never without a cat!

I found Evelyn Underhill a fragile-looking woman with wonderfully alive eyes. When we settled into our visit after tea, we were soon into talk of the mystical experience and its significance, and I had the temerity to ask her to tell me something of her own touch with this transformating gift. She quietly denied that she had any place with those who had had great inward experiences, but added shyly that she had known from time to time what it meant to have "a slowing down."

In the years to come, I read most of what she wrote and recall telling her in a letter, in about 1936, that I thought the finest book she had ever written was *The Golden Sequence*. She answered promptly and said she was glad of this judgment, for it was also her own favorite.

Both of her biographers, Margaret Cropper and Christopher Armstrong, include a fine statement by Barbara Collingwood Gnospelius that describes her as she knew her some years before I met her. It is so vivid that I want to share it with you:

> The astonishing thing about Evelyn in 1916 when I first met her, and when she was already a very well known and respected poet and writer, was her gaiety. She was not certainly an impressive or even a striking object at first sight. She was smallish, stooping, and round shouldered, her clothes definitely dowdy and her hair most unsatisfactory, though even in those days she wore her little lace caplet. . . . But her creased little face, full of animation and very mobile, was an instant attraction; and as I remember it her face was always creased with laughter and twinkling with fun. She had a way of laughing up at you . . . which, while endearing was, to the young and shy, just a trifle daunting. I had expected to meet a lady rather exquisitely withdrawn, but no one could have seemed less lofty and remote than Evelyn or more ready to meet everything and everyone with a bit of a grin, and a sputter of laughter and a naughty irreverent joke. It was most refreshing. We visited her often at Campden Hill Square . . . and we talked about everything, not so much as I recollect War and Politics, as Philosophy, Psychology and Religion.

Evelyn Underhill grew up in a comfortable London home with her father, an able barrister who was knighted, and her mother with whom she was very close. Her father was an avid sailor who had his own boat, and the summers were always full of happy cruises. Hubert Stuart Moore, whom she was ultimately to marry, was the son of a barrister friend of her father's. When Moore's own mother died, he and his brother were much with the Underhills on these cruises, and Mrs.

Underhill was like a second mother to them. Evelyn Underhill went to King's College for Women in London, and became part of a London literary set. She and Hubert Stuart Moore had been sweethearts from 1890 to 1895 and had been engaged to be married from 1895 to 1907, during which years he had established himself as a successful member of the bar. In those Victorian days there was not the pressure that we find in our timing today, and with the perfect security of an ultimate marriage, Evelyn Underhill enjoyed her family, went abroad each year with her mother, and got a full sense of the flavor of France and Italy. During this time she became a highly skilled bookbinder and reveled in a variety of interests like gardening, sailing, weaving, and bicycling. She also had the freedom to get on with her poetry writing and with the publishing of three novels, which were well received.

All her life long Evelyn Underhill had great passion for cats. When she was made a fellow of her own King's College many years later, the Dean included in the citation, "She enlivened her leisure by talking to cats." One was named for a favorite saint, Philip Neri; another was christened Michael Angelo; and even Immanuel Kant was honored by an especially inscrutable pussy whom she called the "Ding an Sich." She always delighted in noting that anchoresses, like Mother Julian of Norwich, while denying themselves almost every human luxury, were nevertheless always encouraged to have a cat. With one of her beloved friends, Lucy Menzies, who had a little dog, there was always some part of the many letters they sent to each other that was devoted to exchanges of greetings and often critical comments of their mistresses from Evelyn Underhill's cat and Lucy Menzies's dog. On one occasion a letter included a review of a book on cats by Evelyn Underhill's cat, David, in which he set down the only kind of home that was suitable for a cat, in which its chair and its meals and its every whim to leave or enter the house took priority over all else! Visitors to the Stuart Moore family reported finding both Evelyn and Hubert sitting before the fire in domestic bliss feeling quite "purry" as Evelyn Underhill would have expressed it, with a cat curled up on their laps. Even von Hügel in a postscript to one of his letters to her writes: "I much like your love for cats. I deeply love my little dog, and the Abbé Huvelin was devoted to his cat. We all three can and will become dearer to God for this love of our little relations, the smaller creatures of God."

Evelyn Underhill did not grow up with religion, although she had the usual British school instruction in the Bible and was what you might have called a dormant Anglican. She describes her own spiritual development as having moved from atheism to agnosticism with the help of philosophy in the early years of the century, and in her novels of these years the strong wistfulness toward a deeper religious experience was evident. She, like Charles Williams, was drawn to explore occultism in these years, but she was repelled by its lust for power without any sign of redeeming love in it. She was described as "an enchanting friend" and had a capacity for deep attachments to her women friends. The most moving friendship after 1906 was one with Ethel Barker who, from a conventional Anglican, had become, like Evelyn Underhill, a hungry seeker after religious reality. This friendship lasted until Ethel Barker's death in 1921. The two went off secretely together for the Easter week in April of 1907 to a French convent of the Poor Clares who kept a vigil of perpetual adoration before the sacrament. Until this time Evelyn Underhill had been ravished by beauty and knew a good deal about spiritual learning as such but had been skeptical of all institutional religion. Her biographer, Margaret Cropper, describes this experience:

> The quiet and peace and the affectionate welcome of the nuns must have been very pleasing to Evelyn's hungry heart, but the atmosphere of perpetual prayer was almost too heady for her. She wrote later to Father Robert Hugh Benson [a most gifted Roman Catholic priest who had converted from Anglicanism to the Roman Church, although his father was at the time the Archbishop of Canterbury]: "I fled after the fourth day, otherwise I should have submitted there and then, as it was it gave me a 'push on' from the effects of which I have not yet recovered. . . . The day after I came away, a good deal shaken but unconvinced I was 'converted' quite suddenly once and for all by an overpowering vision which had really no specific Christian element but yet convinced me that the Catholic religion was true. It was so tightly bound up with Roman

Catholicism that I had no doubt . . . that that Church was my ultimate home."

Ethel Barker, who shared "that wonderful week," went quietly ahead and was received into the Roman church nine months later. But Evelyn Underhill, with her marriage in July approaching, had a lawyer fiancee to cope with, to say nothing of her own intellectual hesitations. Hubert Stuart Moore insisted that to have her bound to go to confession in the Roman church would place another person in the sphere of the marital confidentiality, which for him was too sacred to be broken in this way. She promised him that she would take a year to consider the matter. Three months after their wedding, the pope issued his famous Anti-Modernist Encyclical that led to the excommunication of Maude Petre and George Tyrrell, who were among her favorite writers in the religious field. Her own integrity could not, she felt, permit her to yield to such an institution.

In the years between 1907 and 1911, her drawing back from joining the Roman Catholic church did not keep her from being deeply moved by a study she resolved to make of that church's great mystics and of the whole field of mystical experience as a principal form of human spiritual consciousness. It is an interesting feature of intellectual history to notice how often special facets of our spiritual life will seem to be neglected for a period of time and then a whole cluster of prophetic persons or books will draw them back into focus again. Dean Inge's Bampton Lecture on *Christian Mysticism* appeared at the turn of the century, and William James's *The Varieties of Religious Experience* came in 1902. Friedrich von Hügel's great *The Mystical Element of Religion* was published in 1908 as was Rufus Jones's admirable *Studies in Mystical Religion*. Evelyn Underhill's huge *Mysticism* volume joined this distinguished company three years later in 1911. These books, coming out of very different spiritual traditions and having little to do in stimulating one another, suddenly, in a decade, broke through the crust. Each one from a somewhat different angle elevated the significance of first-hand religious experience, underlining its importance as a renewing and highly important function in the lifting up of persons and the restoring of them to their full stature.

Evelyn Underhill's important book, *Mysticism,* brought her to the attention of Baron Friedrich von Hügel. He was impressed with her gifts in interpreting the mystical life and relating it to the life of ordinary persons, in distinguishing an authentic Christian mysticism from the pseudo-species, and in showing that the great Christian mystics were not content to find peace in the stillness of the Godhead but that, when authentic, their mystical experience girded them with what Ruysbroeck called "an overflowing love for all in common."

Evelyn Underhill published a number of smaller books on mysticism and on mystics of the church in the years following 1911. She was now a marked scholar who was asked to translate or to edit and write introductory essays to the devotional writings of Jan van Ruysbroeck, Nicholas of Cusa, Mother Julian of Norwich, Walter Hilton, Jacopone da Todi, and Bernard of Clairvaux, to name only a few. Her pen had a gay, brilliant, saucy way of making these men and women live again, and she had a perfect genius for apt quotation. She had been writing poetry through the years, and her little volume called *Immanence* appeared in 1912 with its opening verse:

> I come in the little things,
> Saith the Lord:
> Not borne on morning wings
> Of majesty, but I have set My Feet
> Amidst the delicate and bladed wheat
> That springs triumphant in the furrowed sod.
> There do I dwell, in weakness and in power;
> Not broken or divided, Saith our God!

In 1916, the midst of the First World War, she published her second book of poetry, *Theophanies,* which breaks out with the joy of discovery:

> Not to me
> The Unmoved Mover of philosophy
> The absolute still sum of all that is,
> The God whom I adore—not this!
> Nay, rather a great moving wave of bliss,
> A surging torrent of dynamic love

In passionate swift career,
That down the sheer
And fathomless abyss
Of Being ever pours, his ecstasy to prove."

By the time the First World War was over, Evelyn Underhill had been chosen to give the Upton Lectures in Manchester College in Oxford. She was looked to from all sides in Britain for lectures, articles, and book reviews on religious topics, and she was regarded as an authority on the saints. Her married life was happy. Now in her middle forties, she could readily have sailed along on this stream of public and domestic esteem and success for the rest of her days. But she was not content. The life of her dearest friend, Ethel Barker, was ebbing away. More and more people were seeking her out for spiritual direction. Would she fail them? She had a sense that she was called to something deeper than she had yet reached. She had expressed her uneasiness with Inge's book, *Christian Mysticism*, in which he seemed to know all of the right quotations but did not convince her that he had actually been there. Now she wondered if she was subject to the same disease. She knew that she had had breakthroughs in her life when she had felt something greater luring her on, but she still had little place for the role of the historical Jesus or for the institution of the church and the humbling Christian fellowship that it holds out. Behind it all she felt a call to sanctity and to another dimension of life than she had until now discovered. She was encouraged by the fact that her most honored mystic of the middle ages, the Flemish Jan van Ruysbroeck, had had his major breakthrough at the age of forty-nine and that Teresa of Avila was only ten years younger when she was made over from within. There is a climacteric in the spiritual life for both men and women as there is one in the unfolding of the body, and Evelyn Underhill was being made conscious of being given another chance. Sanctity in her eyes had never been a matter of perfection. For her, sanctity was always a condition "where God was having more and more his undivided sway" in a life.

It was at this critical point of yearning and of a sharp midlife despair that she approached Baron von Hügel in the autumn of 1921 and asked if he would be willing to become her spiritual director. They had known each other since *Mysticism* had been published a decade before. She had "sat at his feet" and looked to him as the deepest spiritual figure in the British scene in her day. He had written her of his appreciation for her great book but had, in his inimitable way, after expressing appreciative things about the book, gone on to share his uneasiness about her desire to have the mystics without the church and her failure to realize that "the Church came first and the mystics afterwards." He also was not satisfied at the way she had leaned on naturalistic Bergsonian intuitionism and on the Vital Thrust (Elan Vital) without any real weight being given to the historical revelation that had come in Judaism and in the figure of Jesus Christ as the setting in which Christian mysticism could alone be interpreted. Over these intervening years, she had been facing in von Hügel's great book *The Mystical Element of Religion* his own powerful interpretation of mysticism as one element in a living religion, but as being fruitful only when it stood in creative tension to the historical and traditional element and to the intellectual and critical element. There grew up in her a strong suspicion that she needed to rethink her relationship both to Jesus Christ and to the church.

This pull on her of a life of sanctity also brought a consciousness of how much in herself and in her extremely well-adjusted life resisted this call; how much might have to go. She knew intuitively that without stronger help and guidance than she herself could provide, she would almost certainly sink back into the outward assurances of faith and fail both God and those who looked to her for help. So the friend who wrote von Hügel for aid had, as most seekers have done, already come a long way toward clarification before she ever sought his help and direction. Then, as now, these hunches, these intimations, these preliminary clarifications may still, however, be ever so evanescent and ever so readily lost. What they need is confirmation, the establishment and sinking of roots, the challenging and rephrasing in the face of the challenge, all of which so often can only be affected by reviewing them again before God in the presence of another person. Hence her call for help in this time of crisis.

Her appeal to von Hügel, which confessed that in these war and early postwar years her life had gone to pieces spiritually, brought a prompt and warm reply from him. He seemed to see in this brilliant contemporary of his a woman with a gift for sanctity whom God was drawing nearer by this unsettling that she was reporting. Von Hügel replied with the most open willingness to do anything that he could for her. He told her that he had long been praying for her and longing that she might be readied by God to touch the people of her time with a message that would truly speak to their needs.

From the very outset she had made it clear that she felt no call to move toward entry into the Roman Catholic church and that she had in the last months and years been drawn to renew her roots in the Anglican (Episcopal) church where she believed she belonged. Von Hügel, with her as with all whom he touched, believed that persons should never move from their own religious connections unless compelled to do so in a way that they could not resist. The result of this was that in the next few years, from 1921 to the very time of his death in 1925, von Hügel served as Evelyn Underhill's spiritual director and did much to encourage her in a way of thought and a way of life that would release her to interpret the Christian interior life in all of its richness. I have described this process in documented detail in an essay that I wrote, *Baron von Hügel as a Spiritual Director,* that introduced an anthology that I published, *The Spiritual Counsels and Letters of Baron von Hügel,* where I turned to Evelyn Underhill as a case study. I will say here only that in these nearly four years of guiding her, von Hügel helped to draw Evelyn Underhill into a Christian accent in which the figure of Jesus Christ became more central to her own prayer life and her world view. Christ became for her the expression of the infinite caring for each soul that pours continuously from the ground of being that is the living God. This might be gathered up in saying, "In Jesus Christ, God came all the way downstairs" to the creation. God's poulticelike attraction, this continuous siege of each soul and perhaps of each cell by God's transforming love that is so dramatically expressed in the historical appearance of Jesus Christ, is the ultimate frame in which all Christian devotional life and spiritual growth can be adequately expressed. Why do I pray? Because God first loved me into this most suitable response to the divine caring. What happens when I pray? I become aware of what is already going on in the universe and I join in its operative redemptive action.

About 1927 Evelyn Underhill wrote:

> Until about five years ago I had never had *any* personal experience of our Lord. I didn't know what it meant. I was a convinced Theocentric, and thought Christocentric language and practice sentimental and superstitious. . . . I had from time to time what seemed to be vivid experience of God, from the time of my conversion from agnosticism (about twenty years ago now). This position I thought to be that of a broad-minded intelligent Christian, but when I went to the Baron he said I wasn't much better than a Unitarian. Somehow by his prayers or something, he compelled me to experience Christ. He never said anything more about it—but I know humanly speaking he did it. It took about four months—it was like watching the sun rise very slowly—and then suddenly one knew what it was. . . . The New Testament, which once I couldn't make much of, or meditate on, . . . all gets more and more alive and compellingly beautiful.

This is from her letters. To Dom Chapman she wrote some four years later, "Under God, I owe him my whole spiritual life, and there would have been more of it than there is, if I had been more courageous and stern with myself and followed his directions more thoroughly."

A second accent grew out of these years of von Hügel's counseling. The church, for all of its shortcomings and failures and apostasy, nevertheless in von Hügel's eyes dare not be shunned. Regular exercises of corporate worship cannot be bypassed but must become a part of short-memoried, flesh-and-blood pilgrims who would really let God have sway in their lives. In his quaint way, the baron once reminded his niece that, if ecclesiastical organization offends the angel-like vision of many as to what the ideal church should be, they might well remember that "even Cleopatra, when in the splendor of her youth, had such a very useful, very necessary, quite unavoidable skeleton (bony structure) inside her, had she not?" For him the church is the tarnished mounting in which the jewel of Christ is set. Some years later we find Evelyn Underhill, in a letter of spiritual counsel, putting von Hügel's position unequivocally: "The Church is an 'essential service' like the Post Office, but there will always be some narrow, irritating and inadequate officials behind the counter and you will always be tempted to exasperation by them."

Von Hügel in his spiritual guidance of Evelyn Underhill began with words that would bind her firmly to her fresh return to the Anglican church. He suggested weekly attendance at the Sunday communion and a midweek early service in a convent that was well known to her. For private devotions he suggested no more than fifteen minutes of reading in some good devotional book and, at her stage of unfolding, no more than thirty minutes in meditation and prayer. He suggested that she attend only one retreat a year, but at her suggestion, he extended this to two. Always he recognized that, with her fierce determination to change, she might overstrain herself and the relapse could undo all that had been begun. He suggested that she cut down her extensive religious writing by at least a third and that for the time being she should take on no new cases asking for spiritual guidance. He urged her to find in the ordinary routines of her daily life with all of its unexpected interruptions the real stuff that can quicken the supernatural life. When she complained that intercessory prayer was unreal to her, von Hügel, with real Salesian gentleness, suggested going on with ordinary prayer and hinted that in time, perhaps soon, intercessory prayer would come, as in fact it did. He wrote to her: "We must always thus, in our own efforts, strive to reach what we have not got, by the faithful practice of what we have, although God is in no wise tied in His dealings with us, to this procedure." He suggested the cultivation of some nonreligious interests such as painting or gardening or some craft, but she was already entirely at home in this area. Finally he wrote that, more than anything else he could suggest, to thaw out the cerebral accent in her religion and to break open her heart to the needs of all, she should devote two afternoons a week to "visiting the poor."

Von Hügel noted that nothing would help her to realize more swiftly how little her sophisticated religion was able to speak to the needs of these people and nothing would burn away the fastidious side of her nature more than such involvement inevitably would do. "I would," he wrote, "carefully give the preference to the two weekly visitations (of the poor) against everything else, except any definite home and family duties, or any express wishes of your husband—in each case as distinct from your own likes and dislikes." It was in these visits that she met an invalid, Laura Rose, a woman of the poor who was deeply rooted in life and in what life itself is rooted in, that is, in God. A friendship in the spirit sprang up between these two women across all barriers. She used to say in the moments when she loathed London, "London has one advantage; it holds Laura Rose." This steady visiting of the poor that she kept up for many years only accentuated the social dimension already in her life. She was a keen member of the Conference on Politics, Economics, and Christianity (COPEC), and she gave a major paper at its 1925 session. No mysticism could be tolerable in the Christian frame for her that did not ultimately find its costly witness in the active and channeled love we bear for others. She loved the *Theologia Germanica* phrase about longing "to be to the Eternal Goodness what a man's hand is to a man," and in this COPEC address she writes, "The more purely the flame of contemplation burns, the more is it to be found in the end to inspire saving action. . . . We cannot sit down and be devotional while acquiescing in condition which make it impossible for other souls even to obey the moral law."

In 1924, Evelyn Underhill attended her first retreat at Pleshey, a small Anglican Retreat House located among the wheat fields of beautiful Essex, about thirty miles northeast of London. The usual retreat lasts from Friday in the late afternoon well into Sunday. Pleshey retreatants, in her day at least, kept silence throughout, and this for her was the right climate for inner transformation. There were also services in the chapel, messages from the retreat director, and an opportunity for a personal visit with the one guiding the retreat. In such a two-day regime there was ample time for prayer, for walking, and for consideration of one's life and the course it was taking.

In the years after 1927, Pleshey was to take a central part in Evelyn Underhill's life. The retreat seemed to her a vehicle for quickening the prayer life and for deepening the commitment of those who were concerned for the inward life that she found herself increasingly drawn toward. She became a retreat guide of superb strength. Her beloved friend Lucy Menzies wrote about Evelyn Underhill, "Although she gave retreats elsewhere—at Moreton, St. Edwards, Canterbury, Leiston Abbey, Watermillock, Glastonberry and so on, Pleshey was the first retreat house that she knew and from the first she loved it." It used to be known in the Pleshey neighborhood as "The Holy Land," for a religious house had stood on the place since the fourteenth century and, although swept away by the Reformation, it was later revived as a contemplative community. Lucy Menzies adds, "The ground it stands on is holy ground from which prayer has gone up as incense for hundreds of years. Prayer is its life. Its whole atmosphere invites communion with God." Evelyn Underhill loved the wide expanse of sky and the great fields, as well as Pleshey's garden, its moats, and its moorhens.

Lucy Menzies speaks of Evelyn Underhill's guiding of the retreats of this 1927-37 period:

> There was never anything formal or stereotyped about the retreats that she gave. They were full of life and zest and humor. What she said pierced the heart as when, after allowing some particularly devastating remark to sink home, she would say quietly, looking up, "How do you feel about *that*?" She identified herself with her flock. She was showing them a path along which she herself was travelling, and all of her own discoveries as to the best way, she put generously at their disposal.

Margaret Cropper said of her, "She was a guide who knew her mountain."

Even in the thick of leading such a retreat, Evelyn Underhill never lost her sense of humor. A letter of hers tells of how an old Quaker woman, the eighty-six-year-old widow of Thomas Hodgkin, held her hand and whispered to her during a retreat at Pleshey, "I hope, my dear, while you are watering souls, you get a few drops for yourself." To this Evelyn Underhill replied, "Well, I have to give most of my attention to holding the can!" Her letter goes on to add, "At which she laughed and kissed me."

Speaking of the 1930s, Lucy Menzies writes, "Although she wrote books which opened windows to the Unseen to many, she would have agreed that her chief work in her latter years was the giving of retreats and the 'after-care' of those—and many others—with whom she thus came in contact." It should be added that in the last ten years of Evelyn Underhill's life, her letters of spiritual direction or guidance are among the most precious things we possess of her wisdom in nurturing the spiritual lives of others; and happily, we have a handsome volume of these letters with a fine biographical essay to introduce them. The selection of *The Letters of Evelyn Underhill* was made and the introductory essay was written in 1943, only two years before his own death, by her dear friend Charles Williams. Most of these letters were written to persons who asked her to continue to help them with some guidance and direction. These were people who had come to and been touched by her retreat. No matter how much she was carrying, she seldom could turn away one who seemed to her to have been given her by God for some unrevealed purpose. In these letters there is always accented the return of the person to the "Father's business," which is not very spectacular. "Ordinary life, love, devotedness," she says, "will do very well for the revealing action of God." "Beyond that," Lucy Menzies writes of her, "she was one in whom something Other was found by all sorts and conditions of people. And to a rare degree, that explains why so many went to her for help. She was so easy to talk to, so natural and there was no alarming hint of the scholar and the writer. She was very simple in her life, even in some ways to the verge of austerity."

Evelyn Underhill once said, "The call of those who need us is apt to take us away from what we love to do." Lucy Menzies writes about this spendthrift generosity, "She met all such calls gladly because she cares so much. 'Caring matters most' was a favorite saying of von Hügel's and Evelyn Underhill lived it."

From 1927 to 1933, Evelyn Underhill was the religious editor of *The Spectator*, England's most distinguished journal. She was the wife of a busy professional man and was at home to many distinguished people in London. She wrote articles, reviewed books, and gave lectures to clergy and laity in many different denominations in Britain. She had an enormous correspondence and yet found the time to prepare and give each year a fresh set of retreat addresses at Pleshey, which often became the core of a book. Her choice little book *The Golden Sequence* was first given in a retreat. Apart from her great book on *Worship*, nearly all of the moving books of this period had come in this way. Some of these retreat addresses were published posthumously by Lucy Menzies, her literary executor. In them you feel the contagious fire of the new life that had been born in her in this second thrust that God had given her through the help of von Hügel and of the conquest of the mid-life crisis and the renewal life that she felt she could not withhold from any who were open to it.

Evelyn Underhill suffered, especially in her later years, from severe asthma. Lucy Menzies's eyes made it impossible for her to continue beyond 1938 as the warden at Pleshey. At this time both women withdrew, but their prayer and concern for the place and for its retreats continued faithfully as long as they lived.

The ugly approach and onset of the Second World War clouded the last days when Evelyn Underhill had to take to her bed. She had become one who could no longer reconcile war with the Christian witness, and she wrote in 1938 one of the most moving accounts of the suffering way of reconciliation that I have ever read. She died in the second year of the war. At a memorial service for her in the beautiful little chapel at Pleshey when her memorial tablet was dedicated, this prayer was offered:

> O God who by the lives of those who love Thee dost refashion
>   the souls of men,
> We give Thee thanks for the ministry of Thy servant Evelyn;
> In whose life and words love and majesty were made known to
>   us,
> Whose loving spirit set our spirits on fire,

Who learned from Thee the Shepherd's care for His sheep;
Grant that some measure of the Spirit be received from Thee
may fall on who us loved her.
We ask for the sake of Jesus Christ our Lord—Amen.

Someone said of her, "She was a gateway to God!"

4.

ON LISTENING TO ANOTHER: PART ONE

"On Listening to Another" was first given in London as the forty-seventh Swarthmore Lecture to the British Yearly Meeting of the Religious Society of Friends in May, 1955. Its title in the British edition, published by Allen and Unwin, was Where Words Come From. *It has been reprinted more than once in Britain. The Harper & Brothers edition in the United States, which was published later in 1955, carried the title* On Listening to Another. *Harper & Brothers issued the book again in the early 1960s in a double volume that included an earlier book of mine,* On Beginning from Within. *The lecture has been printed twice since that time but has been unavailable in the last three years. Readers concerned for spiritual guidance have found it especially helpful. In addition to its spiritual guidance, it contains an intimate account of the spiritual insights of the Quaker approach to the Interior Guide. The text has been revised from the original British edition in some places in order to update its language.*

Have you ever sat with a friend when in the course of an easy and pleasant conversation the talk took a new turn and you both listened avidly to the other and to something that was emerging in your visit? You found yourselves saying things that astonished you and finally you stopped talking and there was an immense naturalness about the long silent pause that followed. In the silent interval you were possessed by what you had discovered together. If that has happened to you, you know that when you come up out of such an experience, there is a memory of rapture and a feeling in the heart of having touched holy ground.

Have you ever been writing a letter when your capacity to listen to the other and to that person's situation suddenly comes into focus and all you have been saying or meant to say is swept up into something infinitely more important? You have listened and you have been listened to and you have heard, even though a complete recasting of what you had set down before is now exacted of you.

Have you ever talked with someone who listened with such utter abandon to what you were trying to say that you were yourself made clearer in what you were trying to express by the very quality of that person's listening? Have you ever found this listening changing what you started out to tell and moving it over into quite a different channel? Perhaps you had begun to speak of the loveless character of your own religious group, of how little they cared for each other, and at bottom, how little concerned they were for what happened to each. In the course of telling this, although your listening companion had scarcely spoken a word, it may be that little by little it began to dawn upon you that you were describing not so much the situation of your religious group as the condition of your own heart. Now you began to see what was required of you, and you found yourself reduced to silence. You may have begun by describing your own inner agonies which had been mounting up until they finally blotted out all hope. You had meant to complain bitterly against a fate that had pressed you to such a state of desperation. You had meant to collect a liter or two of sympathy. But as you talked, and as your friend listened with that perfect understanding love which gave you complete attention, the true state of things dawned upon you and you no longer needed sympathy or a towel for your tears. Painful as the insight was, you now saw things from another perspective and you stopped talking. You no longer needed to talk, or if you did continue, it was now on another theme and level.

Perhaps you had sought out a friend to confess something you could no longer keep in the solitary confinement of your own heart. You were not sure you would have the courage to admit how low you had fallen and you began on evasively safe regions, not sure either of yourself or of your friend. But the utter and easy attentiveness, the free and open listening of your friend lifted the latch on the gate and it swung open noiselessly and effortlessly, and all that you had held back tumbled out. Now it was out and now it was over and you had died a little death, but in the patient eyes of the friend which you scarcely dared to lift your own to look into, you discovered that you were still in the land of the living.

Have you had the contrary experience? Have you ever talked to a person on a subject that was of burning importance to you, something that you felt that you must enable that person to feel, and in the course of it had the choking, stifling realization that the person was not listening to you at all, and that any responses to what you said were purely automatic and mechanical? In February, 1941, I went to see one of the highest placed officials in the American government to ask him to use his good offices to soften the wartime American embargo of occupied Europe to the extent of letting some American food get through to southern France where the general population, and particularly the depressed groups like the Jewish refugees and the refugees from Franco's Spain, were slowly starving to death. I had just returned from this region in France and had seen these people with my own eyes, and I tried to help him to see what our embargo was doing.

I had only begun speaking when he apologized and reaching for his telephone asked his secretary to make appointments for him with certain senators. He jotted down things on his pad that had nothing to do with our interview. I faced his body. He said "yes" and "no," now and then. But his mind was elsewhere. He had no interest in this concern. I was unable to draw his attention to its relevance. I went away sad and chastened that I had not been given the grace to draw him to listen.

More often the situation is not so crass as this. The listener is involved in the conversation but only to the degree that the listener is eager to give an opinion. Someone listens to what is said only sufficiently to inject a personal, already-fashioned view at the earliest possible moment. This is listening only with the outer ear. With the rest of the mind, the listener is preparing another speech. In this situation there is no real listening. We have only two tangential monologues in process and neither person is in the least affected by the exchange.

LEVELS OF LISTENING AND THE PRICE THEY EXACT

In order to listen discerningly to another, a certain maturity is required, a certain self-transcendence, a certain expectation, a patience, an openness to the new. In order really to listen, there must be a capacity to hear through many wrappings, and only a mature listener, listening beyond the outer layer of the words that are spoken, is capable of this. How falsely a listener may construe what we say if only our words are taken. Our words are often halting and many times plainly not what we mean. Back of what we mean on the conscious level, there is almost aways a deeper unconscious meaning that is at work.

A young minister in his first year of service tells his friend that he cannot bear the work and wishes he would find a place for him with some good farmer. Does he mean that he is not strong enough to stand the nervous toil that the work of a busy minister of the gospel involves? Does he think that he really is meant for agricultural work instead of the ministry? This is what his words have indicated. But in all probability he means neither the one nor the other. What does he mean? Only the listener who cares and who has the patience of caring and the faith of patience will ever know. In the presence of this understanding patience, the young minister is soon telling that what he really means is that there is no letup to grief in this work, no limitation to the hours he is on duty, and that he feels utterly inadequate to the troubles people open to him, the faith they have in him, the opportunities that are about him night and day, and he wonders if he can ever measure up to them. If the truth were known, you could not drive him from the work. Underneath in his hidden life, he senses that the noose of his own commitment is tightening and is closing around more and more of his life as he is being drawn into a situation where there is less and less chance to extricate himself, hence the above-surface ripples of what in words are complaint, but what in truth are signs that the calling he has chosen is taking him over. The harness is beginning to tighten as the pull of the wagon behind makes itself felt.

What old veteran in religious service has not confided to a companion that the job's grief will not be borne anymore! We often want to quit and look out for ourselves for while. The Curé d'Ars ran away periodically from his parish and his twenty-hour-a-day vigil in the confessional only to return promptly when the parish sent some peasant parishioner after him, as they always did. What parties to a marriage have not at moments had their long thoughts, "All for you, and nothing for me," as the music-hall ballad puts it. What occupation has not at moments looked less attractive to one in the midst of it than other careers around it? But the patient listener soon finds that these "moments," so vociferously described, are not really what the person is meaning to say at all. The listener knows that at heart the speaker is trying to say what even the speaker does not yet consciously know, namely, that the marriage needs another child, or another level of understanding or tenderness. The occupation may need a fresh dedication or another set of undertakings to change its aspect. The shoemaker may need a fresh vision of what this service means to those who go through life shod by such an artisan. But these unconscious meanings are only dimly felt by the speaker and they do not formulate well in words. Complaints and threats are so much easier to express. Only before an open listener do they disclose what they really mean, do the complaints and sighs give way to further understanding.

A Finn once suggested to me that in every conversation between two people there are always at least six persons present. What each person said are two; what each person meant to say are two more; and what each person understood the other to say are two more—there is certainly no reason to stop at six. For the listener of fathomless depth who can go beyond words, who can even go beyond the conscious meanings behind words and listen with the third ear for what is unconsciously being meant by the speaker, this fashion of attentive listening furnishes a climate where the most unexpected disclosures occur that are in the way of being miracles in one sense, and the most natural and obvious things in the world in another.

THE SPECTATOR LISTENER WITHIN THE ONE WHO SPEAKS

This favorable climate for self-disclosure is a rare situation. For in all that has been mentioned, it is in the mind and heart of the speaker that the disclosures must finally come, and these disclosures come strangely enough because there is not only a listening friend sitting near, but because there is also a spectator listener within every speaker that listens while the speaker speaks. That inward listener seems able to grasp what is going on at all levels at once so that it hears the words, it hears the conscious meaning of the words, and it even hears in a throbbing but inarticulate way the unconscious meaning of what is being spoken of, and all three of these simultaneously. Without this inner unity, there would be no possibility of self-disclosure, no breaking through of the hidden unconscious meaning into the speaker's conscious life.

There is a great shyness, a profound reticence about this inward spectator listener. It is acutely tuned to the situation in which the speaker is engaged in speaking while another listens. It is tuned, however, not only to these levels within the speaker and to the speaker's sincerity in what is being said. Curiously enough, it is also focused with almost equal intensity upon these different levels within the person who is listening. What is going on in this person's conscious mind, as well as what is occurring in the unconscious, is never fully veiled to the speaker's inward spectator listener. Is it any wonder then that disturbances in the person who is listening that escape completely the most delicate outward seismographic recorder may yet profoundly affect the situation of self-disclosure of the speaker? And is it any wonder that this favorable climate for self-disclosure is so rare?

For in what listener is there the constant abundance of charity, which springs from the depths of the unconscious and floods and illumines the conscious intelligence and understanding, that makes the listener a tuned and concentrated instrument able to reach through the words and even the conscious meanings of the words to the unconscious meaning of the friend who is speaking, and able to answer to it?

In what listener are there not vast stretches of bored inattention when the listener rests, or tries to rest, or wonders when, if ever, the speaker will subside? In what listener are there not temptations early in the conversation to classify what is being said, to label and file it, and once in this frame, to give it only such attention as this frame calls for? There is then no longer a person before the listener, but a type. There is no longer a creative unconscious solution that neither speaker nor listener sees but that could be disclosed if they reached the depths out of which it might come. There is now only a predictable automaton before the listener whose symptoms and course of development this person is all too familiar with.

In how many listeners is there not some adverse judgment on what is being revealed, some comparison between the listener's own standard of assessment and that of the one who is speaking, a judgment which places the speaker at a point of a scale to be neatly sealed off from the listener? In what listener is there not aroused by some remote congruity with what the speaker has mentioned a compulsion to impose upon the speaker a detailed account of the listener's own personal experiences?

In what listener is there not, upon listening to another, some involvement of personal unconscious meanings and intentions, some stirring up of private, unfaced fears, evaded decisions, repressed longings, or hidden aspirations that flare up and involve the listener so completely that the listener is scarcely aware of the speaker any longer? This may not be a negative reaction. On the contrary it may indicate that the listener is alive, is involved, cares, and has begun to speak whether a word is uttered or not. But this inward speaking of the outward listener, genuine and moving as it may be, unless it is in the same direction as the speaker's concern, may become an intrusive force in the situation.

There is no need to detail the role of the professional listener who, having studied a recent technqiue by which one does not involve oneself but seeks to act exclusively as a resonant Swiss valley, sends back an accurate echo to the speaker of what has been said and leaves the rest to the speaker. Happily, few professional listeners are capable of any such total impassivity, and those that are manage quite readily to uncover the mechanical character of their services to those who visit them. Yet in all of these situations that have been described, the rarity of the favorable climate for listening bears down even more formidably as the grounds for it become more apparent.

If all these deficiencies on the part of the listener were heavily cloaked from the speaker and only rarely detected, it would be one thing. But as has already been noted, the vigilant inward spectator listener in most speakers never relaxes its surveillance. There is little in the outward listener that it misses. And when the outward listener is not really open, there is usually a closure effected in return in the speaker, a watering down to the conventional level as a safety factor is invoked, a self-preservative function that allows no more than surface exposure. Now we begin to realize what "holy listening" involves, how it differs from what passes for listening, and some of the diseases that afflict it.

THE TRUE LISTENER IS VULNERABLE

But we have not yet plumbed it. We have still to look at this condition of openness in a genuine listener which the inward spectator listener in the speaker so swiftly recognizes and responds to. This is a condition that opens doors in the speaker, that brings the climate for self-disclosure, a situation in which the deepest longings in the heart of the speaker feel safe to reveal themselves, an atmosphere in which nothing needs any longer to be concealed. The truth of the matter is that there are no perfectly open listeners. Yet in those who approach this degree of openness, it is clear at the outset that they are involved. In some way I, the speaker, matter for them. Neither of us is a ventriloquist's dummy for the other. Both of us affect each other and cannot come out of this encounter unscathed. Even the professional physician admits that the best work can only be done when the patient feels important to the doctor. The practice of old Dr. Wooster in Waltham, Massachusetts, who would turn his calls over to an adequate assistant and serve with his own hands an old patient who was dying, relieving the nurse of the most menial and loathsome tasks, is a symbol of this involvement. The speaker matters to the listener. The listener is vulnerable. Behind any words of the speaker, there is a quality of life which shows that this is the case.

The genuine listener must not only care. It greatly assists the openness if the speaker knows that the listener has also been through some testing that is comparable to the speaker's own. When Father Damien on Molokai, after years of energetic service to the lepers there, began his sermon in the chapel one Sunday with "We lepers," a new note of reality entered his relationship with the community. When at her missionary hostel in England, Florence Allshorn listened to countless forloughed missionaries telling of their inner numbness after years of taxing duty on the field, they knew that she had once been one of them and that they could be sure they were not simply being ridiculous or betraying the name of the exacting vocation they had chosen. The help that is given by members of the Alcoholics Anonymous to each other; by newly founded bands of alumni of mental institutions to those who have just come out; by parents who have lost children of their own through cancer and who make themselves available to parents whose children have newly entered the hospital and who are facing the same ordeal; by nurses in tubercular institutions who have been cured of the disease themselves is a clue to how openness is assisted by the assurance of a similar testing on the part of the listener.

In the depression days of 1931 when the merchants and business community of Morgantown, West Virginia, were in a state of utter confusion and despair, a Quaker woman named Alice Davice came into the community to help in a child-feeding program. Soon after her arrival, she was asked to speak at a widely attended luncheon club meeting. In the course of her talk she described to them what conditions were like and yet how much was able to be done in a comparable Russian city where she had worked, between 1921 and 1927, under conditions so infinitely worse than any they were experiencing that it seemed comparatively easy for them to trust this relative stranger with their confidences. Openness is assisted by the confidence that the listener, too, has been through the fire.

ACCEPTANCE, EXPECTANCY, AND CONSTANCY IN HUMAN LISTENING

True listeners extend openness when they accept a person who is speaking, when they relinquish all buffing and finishing operations and take persons as they come. Such acceptance is no toleration born of indifference, but is rather a positive interest in the person, an interest that is so alive that judgment is withheld.

In South Africa a white person who was deeply concerned for the improvement of the relations between the races confessed to me that in the situation there, the disease of racial prejudice was so deep that even people like himself who went about crossing lines had become so self-conscious about it as to cancel out all virtue and meaning from the gesture. He begged me to try to persuade some people, whose acceptance of the other race was so natural and genuine as to be beyond this stage of self-consciousness, to come out to South Africa and by their example to help to make such an attitude contagious. It is that kind of unconscious acceptance to which my friend referred, that a sensitive speaker requires of the open listener.

This acceptance, however, does not wither or dwarf the deep expectancy on the part of the listener for the partially concealed capacities which are within the speaker. At the best, the listener by something that is almost akin to divination reaches through to these capacities in the speaker and evokes them. This very expectancy immeasurably assists the speaker in a response to the listener's openness. When Thomas Kelly came to Haverford College for graduate study in 1914, he sought out Rufus Jones, and under the glow of the unfailing sense of expectancy which Rufus Jones seemed able to direct toward those who visited him, Thomas Kelly, all restraints aside, bared his secret dream that in some way he wanted to make of his life a miracle.

This sense of expectancy in a listener must, however, have a durable quality, a constancy about it in order to have an authentic ring. If it is to vindicate itself, it must reappear again and again, no matter what the evidence against it. It must have an infinite patience grounded in faith in what the person may become. A seasoned well-digger is not put off by the soiled muddy water which first appears in the pipe when a flowing well is struck. The well-digger knows that given time, it will run clean.

Even Mathilde Wrede, a friend of a Finnish prisoner, who went on forgiving and believing when the same ex-prisoner failed her, deceived her and cheated her, not once, but time after time, could testify that only as she held firmly and patiently to the expectation of what that man might become, could her listening matter. Her own confessions of her frailty in this regard are shattering to the rest of us in our humiliation before her patent purity.

But as the circle of these qualities that are all of a piece is rounded, we return to the first that undergirds and nourishes all the rest. It is the listener's capacity to care, to care enough to be involved. For the listener who knows what listening is about, there is a realization that there is no withdrawal halfway. There is every prospect that the listener will not return unscathed. There is no lead apron that can protect the listener's own life from being irradiated by the unconscius level of the one being engaged. A friend of mine who has spent many years in listening admits that in the course of it, he has learned something of what the Bible and the Apostles' Creed refer to as the "descent into hell" and is quite frank in confessing that for him each act of listening that is not purely mechanical is a personal ordeal. Listening is never cheap. Only the listener who can say "for what else was I born" can fulfill this vocation.

BEYOND HUMAN LISTENING

It should be more than apparent after the things that have been said about what open listening exacts from the listener why such listeners are scarce and why they are so deeply prized. To "listen" another's soul into a condition of disclosure and discovery may be almost the greatest service that any human being ever performs for another. But in this scrutiny of the business of listening, is that all that has emerged? Is it possible to set forth the perfect listener without a flash of realization that we have been engaged in something more? Is it blasphemous to suggest that over the shoulder of the human listener we have been looking at, there is never absent the silent presence of the Eternal Listener, the living God? For in penetrating to what is involved in listening, do we not disclose the thinness of the filament that separates persons listening openly to one another, and that of God intently listening to each soul?

In his *Purity of Heart*, Søren Kierkegaard gives an image that compellingly reveals this emergence of the Eternal background in listening from the human foreground. There he is speaking of how a devotional address should be listened to, but his image will illumine the way of listening to all vocal ministry. The natural way to listen to such a message, Kierkegaard suggests, is to consider oneself as seated in the audience and the one giving the message as an actor on the stage. The listener is therefore quite free as a member of the audience to criticize both the content of the message and the art, or the lack of it, in the one who delivers the message. But Kierkegaard insists that this is not the right way to listen. And until it is reversed, the exercise of listening is likely to have little result, no matter how habitually it is practiced. To listen correctly, we must radically shift the roles. Now it is not the deliverer of the message who is performing before me, but I myself am on the stage speaking the part. Now there is only a single listener in the audience. That listener is God. But where in this altered scene has the deliverer of the message been placed? In the wings, where that person belongs. The deliverer of the message has no more than the role of the prompter on the old Danish stage who stood in the wings and spoke over the actor's lines in a low voice so that if the actor missed them at any point, they could be recovered with this assistance.

Kierkegaard could have gone on with his figure if he had chosen to do so and could have indicated that this reversal of roles in listening to a religious message was not alone something that one by an act of personal will could do for oneself. He might quite as easily have pointed out that when a religious message reaches not only the ears but the soul of people, that apparently without any effort of will whatever on their part, this very reversal of roles is precisely what happens within them. The message-bearer has been in the focus of their attention as they have been listening, perhaps even critically listening. Then suddenly the message-bearer drops out of sight and those who a moment ago thought they were the listeners are now face to face with the compassionate presence of the Listener from whom nothing is hid but who, in spite of all, loves and accepts them.

There is no deeper spiritual insight in Kierkegaard's writings than this vision of a person placed squarely before God, the Listener, and he continually returns to it in his works. Finally we shall be alone with God and there will be no hurry. Finally there will be no crowd to hide in, no favorable comparisons with others to draw about us like a protective coat, no more self-deception. Finally we shall realize that we cannot evade God. In walking on the Jutland heath, Kierkegaard had seen great stretches of land without a tree or a bush that could conceal a person. Finally it will be like that. Kierkegaard might well have evoked the witness of the 139th Psalm:

O Lord, thou hast searched me and known me!
Thou knowest when I sit down and when I rise up;
    thou discernest my thoughts from afar.
Thou searchest out my path and my lying down,
    and art acquainted with all my ways.
Even before a word is on my tongue,
    lo, O Lord, thou knowest it altogether.
Thou dost beset me behind and before,
    and layest thy hand upon me.
Such knowledge is too wonderful for me;
    it is high, I cannot attain it.

Whither shall I go from thy Spirit?
    Or whither shall I flee from thy presence?
If I ascend to heaven, thou art there!
    If I make my bed in Sheol, thou art there!
If I take the wings of the morning
    and dwell in the uttermost parts of the sea,
even there thy hand shall lead me,
    and thy right hand shall hold me.
If I say, "Let only darkness cover me,
    and the light about me be night,"
even the darkness is not dark to thee,
    the night is bright as the day;
    for darkness is as light with thee.

. . . .

Search me, O God, and know my heart!
    Try me and know my thoughts!
And see if there be any wicked way in me,
    and lead me in the way everlasting!

Here in the 139th Psalm, a clarified person is speaking. Like the prophet Amos, the writer has had a vision of the Lord standing beside a wall with a plumb line in hand. The writer has recognized the Listener and gratefully abandoned all concealment. Now the psalmist is listened to with a listening that hears as no stethoscope has ever been devised to hear. Now the writer is known not as visualized by self, not as thought of by friends, not as depicted by enemies, but as the true self. And with this has come a wave of liberation. Search me, know me, try me, lead me: these are the stages of disclosure and discovery which the psalmist has revealed. To speak to a Listener from whom it becomes progressively clearer that nothing can be concealed; to talk on and on before such a Listener until our silence answers that of the Listener, until disclosure and discovery come, is a longing that is so universal that it could be called one of the "givens" of all human experience.

CLARIFICATION AND THE ETERNAL LISTENER

How many attempts there have been to portray the stripping, the cleansing, and the final valley of decision which marks this experience of confronting the One who listens. I came across a striking example of this portrayal some years ago in the form of a painting by a German Quaker artist, Eberhard Tacke, who with his little family lives in East Berlin. He has painted a scene where a vision of the crucified Christ appears to three men who stand holding their masks in their hands. The vision has stripped them of this covering. In their freshly exposed eyes there seems to be a mingled look of yearning and of fear: yearning to give what this figure asks of them, fear of what such giving would cost. "Search me, know me, try me, lead me."

The German writer Bergengruen has given a thinly veiled portrait of the listening God in his *A Matter of Conscience*, where the various figures accused of a capital crime painfully unwind their tangled skein of deception and truth before the Prince who knows the truth from the beginning. The clarification of those involved comes about because there is present an incorruptible Listener to whom all is known.

Perhaps nowhere is this condition more powerfully described than in the Grand Inquisitor scene in Dostoevsky's *Brothers Karamazov*. There Jesus Christ appears again in the streets of sixteenth-century Seville, and by his acts of healing is joyously recognized by the common people. He is promptly arrested by the Inquisitor's guard and brought to the Inquisitor's prison to face the Inquisitor Cardinal alone. There the cardinal begins his "I accuse." And there in response to wave after wave of rationalization and self-justification on the course that has been taken by the church in order to correct his original work, Jesus is completely silent. He does not in turn accuse, he does not defend any more than he did before Pilate. He only is what he is, and listens. Slowly his listening penetrates to the core of the cardinal and reduces him to silence. There is a final violent thrust: the threat of invoking the death penalty if Jesus does not go at once.

In Dostoevsky's scene, Jesus then crosses the room, kisses the aged cardinal on his bloodless lips, and disappears. Seldom in any literature has the course of the human spirit when it confronts the Eternal Listener been more magnificently depicted than here. Yet even here, the cardinal has spent himself, has had his own arguments and defenses revealed for what they are in the presence of the silent, patient, all-knowing, all-loving One, but we are not told that he has come to the end of himself. The cardinal has entered the valley of decision but has turned back, or he would have fled in search of his visitor that he might follow him.

In a lighter vein, the gay, saucy, sparkling Italian post-war fantasy *The Little World of Don Camillo* brings Don Camillo regularly before the crucifix to expound, to argue out, and to defend his preposterous and ethically dubious proposals. In spite of the delicate line between humor and blasphemy which this novel often bends if it does not transgress, the course of this unorthodox priest's pleas before the crucified one is intensely revealing. Slowly and surely as he argues, the assurance wanes, the insistence weakens, and the real course is reluctantly but finally seen and accepted. The Listener has silenced and clarified the petitioner until the petitioner yields and is transformed.

With the exception of Bergengruen's symbolic portrait of

the Prince, and possibly even this is no exception, each of these examples has given us a further confirmation that all that we discovered earlier about ordinary listening is even more characteristic of the greatest listening of all. For it is not merely in being perfectly known that the Listener finally brings the speaker to silence and to the discovery of what is the speaker's deepest yearning. It is in being what the Listener is and confirming this by what is done that the Listener becomes something more than a roentgen machine. And what the Listener is in the Christian experience is one that cares infinitely for the speaker. The Listener speaks to the speaker's condition out of a love for the speaker from the beginning of the world.

VULNERABILITY, ACCEPTANCE, EXPECTANCY, AND CONSTANCY IN THE ETERNAL LISTENER

It was this unremitting love of the Listener for the speaker that Pascal was inwardly swept by three hundred years ago on the memorable night of November 23, 1654, and it was this experience which authenticated his declaration that Jesus would suffer in agony for humanity until the end of the world. For one who has listened to another person with a bowed mind and tendered heart, how much is vindicated is inwardly confirmed and made alive by the gospel story of the Listener entering flesh and blood and caring so deeply as to consent to have it stripped from him again in order to arouse people to his infinite caring. Phillips Brooks once said, "If you want to know the worth of a human soul, try to save one." He might as well have said, "try to listen one into life." For to listen, there can be no bottom to the caring for the other. Yet we know that this caring cannot be a verbal affair. It must be sealed by some unmistakable material evidence of vulnerability on the part of the Listener.

Bishop Stephen Neill told once of hearing an Indian village evangelist telling the story of the prodigal son and allowing himself some of the liberties of interpretation which his vivid imagination begged for. The evangelist explained how the prodigal's real change had not come about when he made his own decision in the far country to return to his father. And it had not come about when, to his astonishment, his father had come out to meet him and welcomed him home with loving tears and a feast. The real change of heart had not come about until some days later when, in looking at his father, the prodigal realized in a flash that the father's hair had turned gray since he had gone away.

The Abbé Huvelin once told Friedrich von Hügel that no sermon on the mount, even when guided as it was by the most sublime instruction on earth, could ever have redeemed humanity. When God wanted to redeem humanity, it could not be done by any other means than by God's dying. For God there could be no arranging a cheaper form of convincing the human race of God's supreme caring.

Throughout the experience of listening, this evangelical witness is confirmed again. The speaker's silent demand that the adequate listener be tested by sharing some comparable experience to the listener's own is not left without a witness: "tempted in all things as we," "conceived," "born," "suffered," "dead and buried." How materialistically literal are the words of the incarnation. Yet, without this testing, could the Listener have opened the hearts of all condition of people throughout all the ages and released them to pour out their inmost depths to God in order that under compassionate listening they might come to themselves as the children of God?

The speaker's need to be accepted as an original, as having a personal worth, as one who is above classification and who requires that routine judgment be suspended and withheld is met beyond measure in the Listener. "Our good Lord showed me," Mother Julian of Norwich relates, "that it is his full pleasure that a silly soul come to him naked, plain and homely."

Where is the evidence for unqualified acceptance more complete and convincing than in the figure who moved easily and without self-consciousness among publicans, taxgathers, prostitutes, people who were national and racial outcasts of his own fiercely zealous national community and who in his death between two thieves accepted and welcomed the thief who came "naked, plain, and homely," bidding him to be with him in paradise?

This sense of expectancy that we found furnishing such an important part of the favorable climate which the listener supplies to the speaker has never been more conspicuously evident than in the figure of Jesus. His easy unselfconscious acceptance of men and women seemed always to be linked to this power of divination into what they might become.

Is it possible to exaggerate what this expectancy of the Listener did to the impetuous vacillating Peter, to Mary Magdalene, to the despised quisling tax contractor Zacchaeus, to those who had despaired of ever again having either their sight or sanity or bodily wholeness? He stubbornly rejected their surface appearances. He ignored the nicely calculated probabilities of society's judgment of what one might expect of them. He penetrated even the heavy wrappings of what they had themselves settled for in their lives and pierced through to what in their deepest yearnings they still longed to become. He drew this out, confirmed it, and those we have named acknowledged it and accepted it. He answered expectantly to that of God in each of them and they felt and responded to the quickening.

The constancy of this figure needs little more than mention in passing, it is so transparently evident. The human listener at the superb best aspires to this costly patience, this durable steadiness in faith and expectancy toward the speaker, but lapses so lamentably and so often. Even in the greatest of saints, our mirrors of the active love of God in each generation, how often are these qualities clouded. Even in Francis of Assisi or Teresa of Avila, how given to bursts of despair or exasperation at the conduct of those who go on in their wayward speaking while they must continue listening.

In contrast even to these chosen ones, what constancy is found in the One who revealed the nature of the true Listener. The disciples go out to preach and heal and return to confess their impotency. The populace, like water, rises and falls in its favor toward him. The last night with his own disciples, they are quarrelling over issues of precedence in the kingdom. One of them betrays him. He leaves this little band fearful, scattered, fleeing, and in utter dismay, yet these are all that there are to carry on the work he has begun. His constancy, like a regnant acid, dissolves away film after film of their disbelief until it breaks in upon them that they are the children of God and are called to live joyously together in God's kingdom and to share it with all the world.

Beneath all that has been said of the living Listener, as of human listening, there is no concealing the fact that what in the listener acts most deeply upon the speaker either to release or to bind that speaker is not only the costly things that the listener does, nor is it exclusively what in the depths the listener is. What really matters is rather what the listener *is* in what the listener *does*. This cleanses the situation from the outset by distinguishing it from any pseudolistening which is reducible to some readily transmissible technique that makes no appreciable demand on what the listener is. It also throws light on a strange occurrence in the ordinary listening that people do for each other as well as in the spiritual situation in which each person is open before the living Listener. For while the least semblance of an act of self-conscious judgment on the part of the listener destroys and renders sterile the relation to the speaker, yet there is no denying that there is a kind of judgment going on continually between listener and speaker.

THE INNER ENCOUNTER WITH THE ETERNAL LISTENER

The speaker in the presence of a human listener is never unaware of the judgment of what the listener is upon the speaker's own life, and in turn, the listener's own life cannot resist the judging effect of what the speaker is upon it. Here are fields of radiation that interpenetrate each other and that leave neither party unprobed. Nietzsche in his *Thus Spake Zarathustra* declares incisively that "in one's friend, one shall have one's best enemy,"[1] an enemy that rebukes and judges that which is unauthentic or merely imitative in the friend.

In the listener, then, if a true friend, a true listener, there is inevitably an enemy to much that is in the speaker. But this "enemy" in the listener is not the reintroduction of any level of conscious judgment, any weakening of the listener's complete acceptance of the speaker. This enemy is an effortless, unconscious influence which rises up out of what the listener is in what the listener does. It may be all very well to say as Nietzsche does that "many a one cannot loosen his own fetters, but is nevertheless his friend's emancipator."[2] But the odds are heavily against any such miracle. For it is only the listener whose own fetters, if not shattered, have at least been loosened, who seems able effortlessly to irradiate the level of existence of the speaker in such a way as to move the speaker toward release. Any minimizing of the maturity required of the listener may lead to the most tragic circumstances. Furthermore, it is only the mature listener who without disturbing the listening situation can submit both humbly and fearlessly to the counter radiations of the speaker to which the listener is continuously subjected.

Yet even this does not seem to get to the bottom of the matter. It penetrates to a genuine inner encounter between two friends who speak and who listen to each other, and it rightly draws attention to the searching unconscious interplay which takes place between the deep life of each as they listen to each other. But where it fumbles and becomes confused and unsure of itself is that it leaves out of all account the living Listener who "stands behind our lattices and waits." It ignores the hidden presence, the patient, all-penetrating Listener, the third member of every conversation whose very existence, if it is not ignored, rebukes and damps down the evil and calls out and underlines the good, drawing from the visible participants things they did not know they possessed. The Listener does this not in a conspicuous fashion, as an orchestra leader tones down the brass with a menacing downstroke of the baton or calls forth the strings with a beckoning, pleading upward gesture, but does it more like the quietly permeating influence of a person of patent purity sitting silently in a conversation, saying almost nothing, but whose presence there changes all. The New Testament gives a vivid picture of this in describing the scene on the Emmaus road and at the inn in which the presence of the mysterious stranger on the road and at the table changed all and left the travelers' hearts glowing as it withdrew.

Rarely does this business get itself adequately articulated. Common as the experience is, it seems to take a Bernard of

Clairvaux to lift it up above the threshold of consciousness
and to write of it:

> He is living and full of energy. . . . He has quickened my
> sleeping soul, has aroused and softened and goaded my heart
> which was in a state of torpor and hard as a stone. He has begun
> to pluck up and destroy, to plant and to build, to water the dry
> places, to illuminate the gloomy spots, to throw open those
> that were cold as also to straighten its crooked paths and make
> its rough places smooth.

The living Listener who is "living and full of energy"
seems able to take fearlessly the speaker's own diseased
irradiations, lethal though they may be, to absorb them, and
to transform them. Here is a kind of alchemy by which base
metals are transformed into gold by a reagent whose power is
as lavishly and recklessly poured out upon humanity as it is
fathomless. Jesus' acts of healing, as in the case of the woman
with the issue of blood or the many cases of demented spirits,
seemed to involve just such a fearless interchange of radiations. This healing power he revealed moves in our world
today to those who are wakened to it.

The more we come to realize the extent of the penetrating
influence which our own hidden life and the hidden life of our
friend exert upon each other, the more acutely do we come to
appreciate how inadequately prepared we are to listen, no
matter how mature we may be. The deeper this sense of
humbling inadequacy soaks into our minds, the more open
we are to realize the wisdom of seasoned spiritual guides like
Francis de Sales or George Fox, who both insisted that the
task of all spiritual guidance is to take men and women to
Christ, to bring them to the living Listener, and to leave them
there. With this realization, too, the well-known remark of
Max Chaplin's comes freshly to life; he reflected that all the
deepest friendships ultimately bear within themselves the
seeds of tragedy unless both persons have their lives open to a
power that is infinitely greater and purer than themselves.

The more conscious a listener becomes of the influence of
the living Listener in searching both speaker and listener and
in drawing out both to confirm in the other what is high and to

reject in the other what is low, the more certain the listener is that only the cleansing radiations of an utterly loving and charitable one will do. Human listening then becomes what it is: a previously thin point in the membrane where the human and divine action can be felt to mingle with the least opaque cloud of concealment. The human action can begin at any point, the conversation can start where it will, but if it goes on, the living Listener's presence may almost imperceptibly rise into awareness, and with that awareness the total situation is altered.

THE LIVING LISTENER IN PRAYER AND WORSHIP

How true this experience is of prayer. Prayer may begin as a soliloquy in which a stream of petitions is poured out. "I cannot bear the loneliness of my station. I live alone. I have been cut off by distance or death or estrangement from all persons who care for me. I cannot bear the company of my odious self day after day. Why has such a sad lot come to me of all people? It is wrong and the wrong should be corrected." Until now, this has been the outpouring of a person who feels choked with unhappiness tinged with a downright sense of injustice. There are those who insist that such a petition is blasphemy and should be sternly discouraged and certainly denied a place in the legitimate life of prayer. But such purists happily have little encouragement from either the Bible or the masters of prayer.

When they pray, people have to begin where they are. If they are obsessed and clogged up with loneliness and self-pity and a feeling of injustice, how can they be sincere if they do not pour out these sentiments? Veterans of prayer are not shocked at these things. They only insist that the person persevere, continue in the prayer, pray it through until the foreground becomes aware of the background. For in prayer, real prayer, what someone brings is irradiated by a power that loosens the arms that are carrying all these bundles of defective goods, bent on returning them to the merchant with bitter abuse, and the arms relax, and the bundles fall away, and the errand seems unimportant, in fact ridiculously unimportant. The question arises, "What is God willing to have me learn from this time of aloneness? What new step of yielding is God asking of me now? What can I do for God in my situation?" And the person stops talking and begins to listen. What does it matter how self-involved a prayer or a conversation begins if it beats its way through to such an awareness? For in this tendered openness, the membrane between the soul of a person and the living Listener is almost as if it did not exist at all.

The situation in corporate worship is closely akin to that described in private prayer. The company assemble in order to be made freshly aware of God, of their dependence upon God, of what they owe to God's constancy, and of what focus of life and plans, if they can discover it, God would draw them into. They are nominally gathered to experience these things afresh. In fact, they come heavy with freight and often far from any worshiping frame of mind. They may be cumbered with cares, bruised and shamed at the state of their lives, physically and nervously tired, all in all hard-driven by life. Or they may feel dull, torpid, and stale, sated with the routine of life and of their carefully secured and reserved station in it. Is this any condition in which to come to worship? Would it not be better if they stayed at home until they could get themselves sorted out and come only when their hearts were full and brimming, when they longed to praise and thank and adore God? As with private prayer, only the religious Pharisee dares even to put such a question. For a service of religious worship that is not able to take people where they are and draw them into an awareness of what they secretly seek has a place only on the drafting boards of religious romanticists. Jesus declared, "Come to Me, all who are weary and heavy laden, and I will give you rest" (Matt. 11:28, NASB). If the place of religious worship is not a place to bring the rucksacks of care that are strapped to our backs, we are not likely to appear there often.

A service of corporate worship is for those who are weary and heavy laden; it is for sinners, for apprentices and journeymen as well as master workmen, and what we begin with does not matter. What matters is, are we brought to such a focus of attention that our claimful cares are made aware of being petty chatterers in the presence of the patient Listener?

What matters is, does this awareness of the Listener change their course, reorder them, drop them into the background, and finally reduce them to silence as the worshiper becomes still enough to hear God speak? Newman in his *Dream of Gerontius* speaks of the twin disclosure, the "two pains so counter and so keen" which all Christian experience of worship, at its deepest, testifies to:

> There is a pleading in His pensive eyes
> Will pierce thee to the quick and trouble thee.
> And thou wilt hate and loathe thyself; for though
> Now sinless, thou wilt feel that thou hast sinn'd
> As never thou didst feel; and wilt desire
> To slump away and hide thee from His sight.
> And yet wilt have a longing ay to dwell
> Within the beauty of His countenance.

All exercises of worship, all vocal ministry, all growth of concern find their focus here. Do they serve to bring the worshipers into a corporate attentive awareness of the living Listener? Do they keep the worshipers there until the worshipers have both spoken out their cares and been brought themselves to listen? Do they encourage the "knowing Joy" of dwelling within the beauty of the Listener's countenance together with the inward "quickness" that comes when a person dares "to see myself His friend" as Vaughan and Traherne speak of the silent worshiper in the presence of the living Listener? Like the Franciscan Brother Giles embracing the Franciscan tertiary, King Louis, their looking long and lovingly into each other's faces and then parting silently, no words having been spoken or required but both touched to the quick by the other's presence, a true service of worship should open the worshiper to such a moment. And finally does the service of worship having silenced the worshiper's cares, searched out and purified the worshiper's frailties, and encouraged the enjoyment and adoration of God, bring the worshiper to listen with the whole being for the word that may speak out the meaning of present experience? Will it cause the worshiper to listen for the divine accent or the holding back on an inward leading, for the sense of quickened responsibility for the worshiper's fellows and for "thy kingdom come on earth"? If a service of worship and vocal ministry can draw ordinary men and women regularly into this kind of renewal, they have performed their function.

THE ORDER OF FORMAL WORSHIP IN THE PRESENCE OF THE LIVING LISTENER

When it comes to the apparatus of worship that can renew men and women in attentive awareness to the living Listener, the classical Quaker practice of corporate silent waiting on God seems stark indeed to those who are used to the elaborate forms of a liturgical or even a free church service. I can still remember the heartiness of an Italian Franciscan monk's laughter that resounded from the walls of the tiny refectory at the Carceri near Assisi as he told me over our Easter dinner of the time he had been called to Rome in 1914 to be inscribed and granted exemption from the military, and, being there "not really on church business," had broken over and visited the American Protestant Church in Rome. They had sung hymns, prayed, read from the Bible, heard a sermon and sung again, and then to his utter amazement, it was all over, and the people went home. There had been no mass at all—and they thought that they had had a religious service! He could not see how anything could be more ridiculously funny. I wondered what he would have thought of a Quaker meeting.

It is not what is missing, but what is present that makes this plain Quaker form of corporate renewal so natural and so adequate. For the worshipers are present, and the living Listener is present, and the worshiper's needs are there in abundance, together with the needs of the community and of the world, and the living Listener's magnetic transforming caring is present and able to meet those needs and to draw the worshipers into service. Present also is not only this little company, this fellowship of those who know each other in that which is Eternal, but the spirits of all of the vast company of the faithful, living and dead, whose inward ministrations are not wanting.

The most ardent free or devoted adherent of a liturgical church would be the first to admit that the Quaker type of lay religious fellowship with its worship of silent waiting and its waiting ministry is spared certain problems which afflict their forms of worship. When the late Dean Willard Sperry of the Harvard Divinity School, in what is generally acknowledged to be his finest book, *Reality in Worship,* begins to detail some of the defects and troubles of free church worship with its elements that are "assembled and not grown"; with its "pilfered prayers secured through predatory raids on the liturgy"; its responsive reading of bloodcurdling psalms that cannot but outrage the discerning, or if expurgated of these elements, excite the criticism of the "whole-Bibleists"; its prefabricated sermons; its prayers over the collection; the garbled architecture and the treacly hymns, a Quaker may have some ground to give a grateful sigh. The liturgist, too, with the problems of rote and purely mechanical habits that groove both clergy and congregation, often enough inoculating them with a kind of assured immunity to the meaning and to the costly surrender which the words demand, presents another set of obstacles that are not found to disturb a Quaker service of corporate waiting worship.

But in the conduct of both of these types of public worship, whose frailties their most honest adherents do not try to conceal, it is of first importance to note that there is an objective rhythm, a sequence of outwardly guided exposure of the worshiper to stages in the worship of God that are of deep significance. There is, of course, some minor variation between the practices of denominations, but more striking than the variation are the elements of praise, penitence, assurance of forgiveness, thanksgiving, petition, intercession, vocal message of edification, consecration, and benediction that are common to them all. Assisted by music and some vocal participation on the part of the congregation, the clergy guide them through these movements. These elements are the outward invitations to inward states of soul, to inward stages of experience, which if they laid hold of the worshipers as they are intended to do would bring these worshipers into the presence of the Listener and renew and refresh their lives.

In laying these elements aside as Quakers do in their silent waiting worship, there is a responsibility whose magnitude it is scarcely possible to exaggerate that is placed squarely upon the Quaker worshiper. Here indeed is a service of worship that demands that every believer be one's own priest. For in the Quaker meeting for worship, the member must still the body, still the mind, must attend to the presence of God, must thank and adore God for being what God is, must feel the incongruities in one's own life that are out of keeping with such a presence, must long for their removal and for forgiveness, must be inwardly absolved, must become conscious of persons and situations in special need and draw them into this presence, must wait in utter stillness before God, and, if some even deeper insight into one's own condition should be discovered by any vocal ministry that may occur in the meeting or by the unhurried stay in the presence of the Divine Listener, the member must be ready to yield.

NOTES

1. Friedrich Nietzsche, *Thus Spake Zarathustra*, 1:14.
2. Ibid.

5.

ON LISTENING TO ANOTHER: Part 2

It is sobering to reflect that unless the Quaker worshiper who has laid aside many outward aids used by fellow Christians has learned their interior equivalent and has grasped the gentle art of guiding one's own spirit through such an hour of worship, guiding it in such a way that it can resist outer and inner distractions or can recover from their ravages if the worshiper has succumbed; can draw the worshiper out of the drowsy, day-dreaming, wool-gathering states; can resist what Augustine refers to so tellingly as the state of "dispersion, in which I turned from Thee, the One, and was vainly divided"; can dare to enjoy God and bear what is asked of the worshiper's life as the cost of company in such a presence, this silent waiting worship can disintegrate into a boring state of deadness. It can fall into a situation of vegetative stagnation, or what is more likely, can be replaced by a period of strictly mental effort on a variety of themes that is not to be distinguished from intellectual application in any secular setting. For alas, the silent waiting worship of Quakerism is not above its own catalogue of frailties, different as they may be from those of other Christian groups.

I know of nothing more inspiring than an utterly free school where a truly great educator dares to trust the teachers and pupils to the point where the disciplines become inner ones instead of the usual authoritarian "whistle and bell" type that are imposed. I have visited such free schools under remarkable Quaker educators like the late Per Sundberg. But I know of nothing more tragic than such a progressive school when death or illness or transfer has removed the inspirer of these inner disciplines, when they have been allowed to atrophy away, or when a new generation of students has come in demanding the old freedom but ignoring the inward order that the great pedagogue inspired. The resulting absence of any effective order either inward or outward is not easy to endure.

In the Quaker waiting silence, there is a freedom and an absence of externally guided order which is both baffling and deceptive to one on first acquaintance with it. Only slowly do the inner forms of discipline of this form of worship make themselves known, for too little has been written about them. Friends feel almost as if they were becoming morbid even to examine them, and they seem instinctively afraid to look at this inner order too carefully lest they become self-conscious and in some sinister way their spontaneity in worship be interfered with.

One thing, however, is clear. This type of free worship can only be creative in a company of people who are intimately aware of and intimately gathered round the living Listener who knows all yet cares, who shares, and whose expectation never wavers in its constancy. It was to this that they rallied from the beginning. All of the inner order and discipline is a reflection of that. Without it this free silent waiting worship is unthinkable. And without that at the center these forms of inner order become the cold artificial psychological devices that Friends in their most fearful moments have suspected them of being. The dilemma which anyone seeking to explain Quaker worship faces is that only when this inner ordering has dropped into the background as we are swept up into the presence of the Listener, only when what was willfully and consciously begun has been crowded out of consciousness by something to which it led, can the real significance of the preparation become apparent, and yet by that time this inner ordering seems like trivial scaffolding compared with what has now been discovered.

On deeper reflection and greater maturity, we can, nevertheless, be brought to see that what is consciously and voluntarily done by us in moving ourselves into the silent waiting worship is not to be scorned or ignored. The fact that we gather for corporate worship at all is a violation of complete spontaneity. God is quite capable of laying hold of us anywhere. Why should we gather at an appointed time to seek to become aware of God's presence unless some willful order on our part is called for?

VOLUNTARY AND INVOLUNTARY ATTENTION IN QUAKER CORPORATE WORSHIP

If we go back to the simplest act of attention on our part, we find it contains both a voluntary, self-induced phase, and if the attention is favored, an involuntary phase where the object of attention itself takes over and our own effort falls away. The more I know of a subject, the more experience of concentration I have had, the more support I get for this preliminary stage of voluntary attention and the less difficult it is for me to place myself before the subject. If I want to write a letter, I usually get the materials and sit down at my table and call to my mind the person I am writing to. I may read over thoughtfully that person's last letter. I may think very especially of some things I want to reply to or some experiences of my own I want to share. In the early lines of the letter I may find it hard to get under way. I am easily distracted. I may even give up. But if I stay put, these distractions usually pass and before long I am totally engrossed in this relationship with my absent friend. I have forgotten where I am, what else I have to do, how hard it was to have gotten under way. Then I may emerge and find the letter only partly finished, and again be distracted. In the engrossed phase my attention was given involuntarily. Now I must rely on voluntary attention once again, and I give it. Then another burst of communication comes and I am again absorbed and my attention is wholly involuntary. This may happen several times before I seal up the finished letter.

Does this mean that the fact that I had to use voluntary attention to get placed and under way and again to continue in the breathing patches of my letter is any sign that I do not care for my friend? On the contrary, these voluntary stretches are signs that I am a free person and that I have chosen to spend my freedom on this person for whom I care. Unless I did care enough to use this voluntary guidance, the involuntary stretches would be most unlikely to come.

In the Quaker discovery of an inward order, an inward discipline that would bear a worshiper into the heart of the silent corporate waiting, much can be learned from such a study of the nature of attention. For it is the focusing and refocusing of attention upon the Divine Listener that is the small part which the frail worshiper can perform and which the worshiper must perform if this form of service is to be fruitful. The presence of a group of earnest worshipers is of itself a great encouragement to the individual. But it is not enough. The individual worshiper must do more than come to the place where others have also gathered. The individual must learn the act of voluntary attention earlier as a child brought up in it until it becomes a natural thing to enter into the silence, or if this training has not been adequate or is totally wanting, as an adult.

Those Friends to whom this gift of voluntary acts of attention is second nature would do well not to take it too much for granted in newcomers to the meeting. It was not alone a barrenness in worship and ministry among birthright rural American Friends in the mid-nineteenth century which led to the return of a considerable portion of American Quakerism to the conventional free Protestant type of service led by a pastor. It was quite as much the entry into those groups of persons from other denominations to whom the silent waiting worship was foreign and who were never helped to learn the way to participate in it that led to their adding their voices toward its rejection.

The characteristic reticence of Quakers to speak of these voluntary acts of attention on the part of Quaker worshipers has a further root in their sound realization of the drastic variations in temperament and in personal needs in so intimate a matter as coming into the presence of God. In any suggestions that could be made, it is assumed that the order may need to be changed, there may be some areas that need dropping out entirely, and other forms of help that are not mentioned at all may be especially needed. Yet after all this has been said, and rightly said, there are certain common elements in this matter of taking the spirit by the hand and leading it gently into the presence of the Great Listener and from time to time softly drawing it back there again, elements that should be able to be stated with a minimum of complexity and adornment.

STEPS IN THE PRACTICE OF QUAKER CORPORATE WORSHIP

It can be assumed that having been seated on a meeting house bench, the worshiper's first act is to get Brother Ass, the body, properly tethered and out of the way. Many have found it a help if the legs are crossed at the ankles instead of the knees, and the body placed in a posture that neither strains nor droops into an inert slouch. Kagawa is said to advocate keeping the eyes open in prayer, but most worshipers find that closing them aids concentration.

When this is done, how can a beginning of worship be better made than to remember into whose presence we come; "Draw nigh unto God, and he will draw nigh unto you." Some years ago, I was asked to go to Lambaréné to visit Albert Schweitzer. I had heard him speak and play the organ at Oxford when I was a student, twenty-five years before, but I had never met him personally. In the meantime, he had come to embody for me much that was most admirable in our time. I suppose that I would rather have met him than any man living at that time. Yet as I approached the Lambaréné hospital, coming up the Ogowe River in a small boat, my heart was so full I was almost fearful of the meeting. I was thankful for the climb up the steep path before we got to the building in which he had his room. It seemed especially good that we did not have to hurry. For to prepare to go into the presence of such a man, one wants to be inwardly tidied up and ready. I wanted to be inwardly quiet and open when I met him, and not with loose, random talk on the lips. If such a feeling is authentic about meeting a great contemporary, how much truer is it of coming into the presence of the living God?

DISTRACTIONS AND THEIR CONTROL

To keep recalling the greatness of God whose cosmic ordering of the infinite spaces is as fathomless as the divine love, and to prepare to sit quietly in the divine presence here and now in this company of worshipers, is not only a helpful exercise in entering the silent worship but one that again and again as outer or inner distractions draw at our minds, is a positive restorative of telling strength.

Most Friends know how worse than futile it is to fight against distractions or to feel despondent at their presence as a sign that they are not fitted for this form of worship. There is no noise-free meeting-place. There are no persons, no matter how saintly, who are not subject to persistent mental distractions. These noises and these inner mental intrusions are a part of our outer and our inner lives that are simply there. If accepted, acknowledged, and quietly ignored as we move on into worship, they fade into the background. Some prefer to enfold outer distractions into a prayer, "O God, may my heart wing its way as swiftly to Thee as the flight of the jet plane whose moan has punctured our silence." "O God, kindle in our hearts here and now a childish joy that will match that of those gay playing children whose shouts we have heard," and with this they get on with their worship.

Some find it helpful to ask God what this mental distraction, if it is persistent, is really able to communicate to them, what unfaced fear, what unfulfilled obligation, what leading into greater faithfulness is concealed in it, and then find themselves back in God's presence having been opened even more deeply to God's will by this intrusion. Most Friends, however, acknowledge and ignore these distractions, leaving them to furnish a cloud frame over their worship but one to which their attention is not centrally directed. As they quietly return to the center, these distractions may even have served to renew their naked intent to yield themselves to the presence of God.

It is a rare Friend whose own personal needs do not operate to draw inwards when a beginning in worship attention has been made. The Listener hears the language of the heart that often has much to tell: the infidelities of the week, the decision still pending, the heart of stone, the withheld consent. In the Listener's hearing, how differently these things appear! How far from the mark! How deep the abyss! Mercy, forgiveness, a fresh approach are required. Such silent worship is not for the good, if there are any. It is for sinners. Before the Listener, how clear beyond a shadow all sin becomes, yet the forgiveness is already given before it is asked. The healing is there, even the strength for the renewal, for the ignition of this supposedly non-inflammable person. "The light that shows us our sins is the Light that heals us." But this light is no sun lamp. It is an X-ray beam. It is deep therapy.

THE ROLE OF ADORATION IN WORSHIP

Thankfulness for such a Listener's ministrations is something many Friends find a natural response to the occasion. This is not a mere counting of one's blessings, although that is an exercise not to be sneered at. It goes deeper, however, and there is thankfulness for the Listener, for the Listener's love, constancy, caring, for being what the Listener is. It is at this point that regular touch in private with the Bible and a fresh sense of the meaning of Jesus' life and ministry and death and resurrection and inward accessibility can furnish a reminder of countless grounds for gratitude. This can also pierce the torpid envelope around the worshiper's soul with a sense of how much God cares. Thankfulness at this level passes readily into adoration, into the quietness of which Fox speaks when we are instructed to be "still and cool from our own thoughts," simply open-hearted at being in the company of the living Listener. We are known, we are accepted, we are thankful to be silent before God. The psalmist's "Search me, know me, try me, lead me" are all laid aside. We do not want gifts. We want only God. We want only to enjoy the divine presence.

Yet in this presence, in this very enjoyment, there is no snug coziness. In the adoration of the Listener, we find ourselves always quivering before a mysterious depth that we cannot get to the bottom of. The traditional spiritual declares: "God is so high, you can't get above him. God is so low, you can't get beneath him. God is so wide, you can't get around him." The experience of adoration confirms this. If in a friend or in one we love there is always a final solitude, a final depth that we forever approach but never penetrate, is it surprising that, in the living God, we find an abyss of being that in adoration brings us into a mingled sense of awe and of glad creatureliness? How good to be the creatures of such a creator, the branches of such a vine, the friends of such a Friend!

CORPORATE WORSHIP AND THE REDEMPTIVE COMMUNITY

But Quakers enter the service of silent waiting not alone or in a series of separate reveries but in a company of worshipers. They know something of the needs of their fellow worshipers; they know something of the sufferings and needs of the world. Often they are conscious of a whole redemptive company of faithful departed ones who are engaged in this all-embracing struggle as well. This realization and these needs are gently brought into the worship in the form of intercession, of bothering the souls of others. "We must be saved together, we must come to God together. Together we must be presented before Him. Together we must return to the Father's house," Charles Péguy has his *Joan of Arc* declare. Often Friends have been able to cross the threshold into true worship in bringing into the Listener's presence the needs of others rather than their own. But if I do not know my fellow members, if I do not call on them, if I am not concerned for them, if my mind and all of my personal resources are not at the disposal of both near and distant situations of need at other times, this leading of the spirit to bring before the presence of God these needs has neither sincerity nor deep intent behind it.

William Russell Maltby, speaking of his own prayers of intercession, says he heard through them a voice that queried, "How long hast *thou* cared for him?" Often in intercessory prayer we are brought to realize how little we care, and how much God cares, and how lightly we had asked for "the ordination of the pierced hands." But in this very insight we are suddenly before the Listener again and we have been stabbed by the painful realization of how long God has cared.

There is finally an offering of what we are and what we have to the Listener, a holy pliability, an inward agreement to the one thing needful, a waiting on God for some accent, some quickening that will draw us more usefully into the intricate skein of human relationship in which each of us stands. To leave a meeting without this offering is to leave too soon.

Now in speaking of these voluntary acts of attention that Friends may well learn how to apply inwardly to their own spirits as they sit in a corporate waiting silence, the acts of aspiration in remembering into whose presence they come, of penitence, of thankfulness for absolution, the acts of adoration, of intercession and consecration, and of openness to concern, we have been speaking of those little-mentioned inner disciplines which this free form of religious worship asks of its participants. But these inner disciplines have all presupposed the active moving presence of the living Listener. And the Society of Friends needs nothing as much today as a fresh baptism of inward realization of who it is that truly sits at the head of the Meeting.

THE GATHERING THAT IS BEYOND VOLUNTARY ATTENTION

The gentle inward leading of the mind by the Quaker worshiper over the ground which in outward symbols and words is faithfully patrolled by our fellow Christians in their services of worship is immeasurably assisted when again and again what is begun as a voluntary, subjective act of guided attention on our parts is lifted from our hands, and our souls wheel through this course drawn irresistibly by the living power of the all tender One whom we confront in worship. Then we know inwardly what Angelus Silesius meant by his Christian imperative, "Bloom, frozen Christian, bloom. May stands before thy door." What we have done, and rightly done inwardly in the way of gentle leading, of praying, is both superseded and confirmed. The Russian orthodox Saint Seraphim of Sarov could not have put more simply what the experience of Quaker corporate worship has learned: "We must pray only until God the Holy Spirit descends . . . when he comes to visit us, we must cease to pray."

It is good to come to the Friend's house of worship. It is good to have remembered God very especially at this time and to have brought my body and my mind and all I possess to this celebration in God's honor. It is good to have placed myself quietly in the presence and to have remembered all that God has done for me, all that has been done for others, all that God does for the cosmic universe, and to have opened my needs and the needs of the world to this One. But how infinitely better it is when in the course of this, I and my fellows feel ourselves brought low, tendered, renewed, strengthened, and perhaps even commissioned to take a step that we might have ignored or hesitated over had this occasion been wanting.

Now there is no contempt for having learned the inner guiding that brought us to the Listener's presence. Now there is no confusion of these rehearsals with the performance itself. Now there is no scorn for the outward practices of other groups. There is only the query: "Did you finally find the Listener taking over? Did the Listener clarify your speech? Bring you to insight? Were you at last silent before the Listener, broken and silent, and yet joyous and infinitely grateful?"

WHERE WORDS COME FROM IN FREE VOCAL MINISTRY

No mention has been made in the description of the corporate waiting silence gathered inwardly by the living Listener of the part which vocal ministry plays in the Quaker service of worship. Luther once declared, "Where God's word is not preached, it would be better that no one should sing or read or come together." If this were to be taken literally as referring to vocal ministry, Quakers would repudiate it vigorously. For the meeting for worship can and occasionally does conclude without any offering of vocal ministry at all, yet with the word of God so mightily preached in the hearts of the assembled company that few present are not touched by it.

Quaker experience repeatedly verifies the fact that without any outward preaching, the corporate silent waiting on God can of itself become a crucible where the slag is separated from the pure ore and where precious metal is refined and cleansed. Again and again such a worshiping company has been baptized into a feeling sense of "where words come from" and has been spoken to directly by the Word and not by words.

One of the tragedies of formal Protestant services is their wordiness, their forensic character. It is so easy for Protestants to confuse the Logos, the Word which God speaks to the heart of the world, with the words of the preacher. When Jesus gave his command, "Go ye into all the world, and preach the gospel" (Mark 16:15, KJV), it is highly doubtful if he had a global speaking tour in mind. In his own ministry, healing and prayer, friendship, common meals, common festivals and even his final decision to die, all give the appearance of having been in his estimation on a level quite comparable to his speaking. Stanley once declared of Livingstone, "He made me a Christian and he never knew he was doing it."

There is an old story of a boy who joined the Franciscan Order longing to become a friar preacher. He was put to work in the kitchen for the first months and got more and more restive and inpatient to get on with learning to preach. Finally Francis himself drew him by the arm one day and asked him if he would like to go into the village with him to preach. The boy's heart was full as they set out. They stopped on the way to see a man whose son needed work in the town, then to call on an old woman who was sick and lonely, and to visit with a peasant at work in his fields. In the town, they saw a merchant about a post for the son, they begged some food for the brothers at home, they talked with some people in the market place, and then Francis turned to the boy and gaily proposed that they return to the friary. "But when are we going to preach?" asked the boy in an anguish of concern. Francis slipped his arm about him and said, "Why my brother, we've been preaching all the time."

When all of this has been said, however, and Friends have always had a very special tenderness for the forms of ministry that are executed in deeds rather than in words, it cannot be denied that both Jesus and Francis did try to convey, in the precious vehicle of human communication supplied by words, what God's love and caring was like. But both were men who knew silence. Jesus by night, Jesus in the desert, Jesus on the mountain returned to silence. Francis on the middle slopes of Mt. Subasio or on the jagged Bibbiena hills at La Verna did the same. Theirs was a speech that came up out of the silence, the silence before the living Listener where their lives were being continually renewed and restored. Their words were rimmed with this silence, with this presence, and therefore they carried an authority and a power that contrived, detached words never possess.

A highly respected German philosopher, Martin Heidegger, in a happy phrase refers to language as "the dwelling place of being." Language is indeed the foreground of reality, its articulate shore. But back of language and clinging to it, when it is real, is the receptive sea of silence. Language is always tempted to make reality more articulate than it is. And the words of language are always being rebuked and overrun and swallowed up again by the silent ocean of existence from which they once emerged. It is obvious that without some form of language, existence would be hidden and mute, but only when words come up fresh and breathless, come up still moist and glistening from the sea of existence, do they carry power and authority.

If this is true, it cannot surprise us that words made from other words, books written from other books, sermons preached from other sermons lack this authentic ring and power. Language torn away from the background of silence, of existence, becomes stale, emaciated, and powerless. When words speak to the center of existence in a listener and call for a recasting of life, they must have come freshly out of the same center of existence which the speaker has touched.

At no point is this more patently self-evident than in vocal ministry. Bede Frost in his *St. John of the Cross* goes as far as to say, "The exercise of preaching is spiritual rather than vocal. For although it be practised by means of outward words, its power and efficacy reside not in these but in the inward spirit." He goes on to add, "It is a common matter that so far as we can judge here below the better is the life of the preacher, the greater the fruit is produced." There is an old adage that declares, "A holy priest makes a perfect people; a fervent priest, a pious people; a decent priest, a Godless people. Always a degree less of life in those who are begotten." In these remarks about the preacher's life, the reference seems to be to the issue of whether the preacher's "inward spirit" comes from the source of power itself. It is as if the preacher, like a disc of cobalt, could only beam through diseased tissue and radiate healing after having been long in the atomic pile and having become a transmuter of what was received there. The Quaker insistence that vocal ministry which occurs in its corporate silent waiting worship shall first grow up out of the hidden life that is moving in the meeting and that before it is released it shall be held in this life, shaped in this life, and confirmed by this life, is an expression of the same temper.

This relation of words to the Word has been a central problem for Quakerism from the beginning. For it soon enough became clear that a meeting for worship that was habitually "starved for words," habitually silent, tended to wither and dwindle. A Swiss writer, Max Picard, suggests that "the perfect silence is heard to echo in the perfect word." In a meeting for worship, in spite of exceptions, the silence is likely to be most vital when it is not habitually mute but when it comes to fruition in vocal ministry and in turn enfolds this ministry in the laboring silence which follows.

This normal expectation of vocal ministry on the part of a lay body like the Quakers has profoundly tempted it at periods in its life, and in the last half of the nineteenth century went so far as to lead one large group in the Society to secure such ministry by engaging professional ministers to supply it, as is done in other denominations. This same expectation in the silent waiting type of worship has also had the effect of tempting some of its members to speak words that have lacked the inward baptism that was spoken of above, resulting in a chatty, conversational type of contrived homily or the word of ethical counsel directed at the worshiper's conscience. There has never been a time, however, when some flash of the strain of prophetic ministry has not been present to reverse Gresham's law that bad money drives out the good. This prophetic ministry has had an authentic mark about it and while its leafy structure has altered from generation to generation it has been marked by a common stem.

A CORPORATE LISTENING SILENCE AND A PROPHETIC MINISTRY

What is that common stem? What is the common trait that characterizes a prophetic ministry and makes the varied accents of the generations fall away before its invariableness? A prophetic ministry is a listening ministry. It has learned what is meant by "Listen before you speak, see before you say." Because it is a listening ministry, it is a ministry that has come freshly from a firsthand experience of the good news it proclaims. It has been preceded not, as in most services, by a period of worship on the part of the congregation with the minister carrying through a professional routine in the prescribed way. Here there is no longer a division of minister and worshiper.

In this Quaker mutation, ministry has been preceded by the whole company, including those who may minister, being gathered in worship and the very ministry rising up out of this listening silence. Here the living God has listened this organ of the gathered meeting into a condition of openness. The meeting has been listened into a readiness to receive. It has been listened into a corporate drawing toward the loving One whose presence can reconcile all enmity, melt all hatred, and kindle into active love every power that seems to resist it.

Here is the common stem that George Fox and Isaac Penington in the seventeenth century; John Fothergill, John Woolman, and Job Scott in the eighteenth; Thomas Shillitoe and Stephen Grellet in the nineteenth; and John Wilhelm Rowntree, Rufus Jones, and John William Graham in our own time, in spite of the vastly different accounts of the human mind which they might have given, could all have agreed upon.

A BALANCE SHEET ON QUIETISM'S ANSWER TO WHERE WORDS COME FROM

The most extravagant eighteenth century Quaker Quietist who sought to treat the mind in worship and in preparation for ministry as a *tabula rasa,* as a blank sheet of paper or as a hollow tube, a horn through which God could blow, becomes less unintelligible to us today if we recognize what this Quietist was protesting against. It was a ministry of words, a ministry that had not been freshly tempered, hammered out, and reshaped in the powerful forge of the silent listening meeting. Quietists were pleading instead for longer and more attentive listening to keep the forward, wordy part of themselves back and to be penetrated by the all-searching, all-transforming presence of the eternal Christ who could be met only in that way. They were asking those who lead others to stay seated in that presence until their own frosted hearts were melted down and they were fused with the needs of those immediately present and of those everywhere who suffer. These people rightly sensed that it was not words alone, or the minister alone, but rather a hidden part in the worshiping minister that is called out and quickened in the course of the group-listening to speak to the hidden part in the minister's fellows.

Job Scott, who, like John Woolman before him, died in middle life of smallpox while on a foreign journey in the ministry, was one of that Quietist company. Of his own witness, a memorial minute from the Meeting in Dublin, Ireland, that is attached to his *Journal* says: "He was a diligent waiter to experience renewed qualification to service, before he attempted to move either in ministry or in the transactions of the discipline; as well knowing that without a fresh anointing, any endeavours to act must prove effectual and tend to a lifeless formality: against which he was zealously concerned to bear testimony."

To read the journals of such as Job Scott, John Fothergill, or John Cunningham, to name only three, is to come into a fresh realization of how much they have to teach us about unhurried waiting in the presence of the Divine Listener, of waiting until the surface mind has been stilled and the deeper levels of our being are drawn out. Such a reading, however, will not close our eyes to the need for prizing more highly than they do the gifts which the Quaker worshiper brings to the ministry, nor will it tempt us to belittle, as they did, what these gifts in God's keeping can contribute to ministry.

It would seem that the principal ground for this Quietist error lay in their curious psychology that failed to distinguish between an inward clarification in which the ministering worshiper was indeed given an insight to be shared, and the different levels on which this insight might be searched and communicated. Failure to distinguish between these resulted in the first place in a radical depreciation of all natural and cultivated gifts which the ministering worshiper might lay in God's hands for use in searching and communicating this disclosure. It also ignored the results of all previous dedication. Such a ministering worshiper may have been brought to live by the hour and the day and the year as one who was more and more attentive to "the pulses of the divine whisper," and therefore may have arrived at the meeting for worship so prepared that when the worshiper had felt the inward exercise of the meeting, and when the Divine Listener had brought the inward conversation to clarity, the worshiper's mind and life presented a supple instrument that was fitted to search and to share this insight in such a way that the hidden power of God could charge the words used.

LAYING THE FIRE IN VOCAL MINISTRY

To admit freely that the precise words, the illustrations, the capacity to quote scripture, or the telling lines of some poem have been drawn from the worshiping minister's lifetime of preparation is in no sense to minimize the source of the insight which these words are used to search and to communicate. George Fox was an assiduous student of the Bible and knew it almost by heart. The mighty works of God recorded in scripture were always before him and this knowledge was always at the disposal of the inward insights that were given to him. Fox was also a man of prayer, a man who was "energized in secret for life in the open world." By being continually open to inward guidance, the exercise in the meeting for worship was a natural one for him and he came to it attentive and inwardly gathered. The practice of regular prayer and a continual intent to listen for the deeper meaning in everything that happens in life is an indispensable preparation for this type of ministry.

It is said of John Woolman that he was a hard reader all his life and his ministry and writings reveal an appreciation for and a discernment of the views of others that reflect this form of outward preparation. Bonaventura, when asked by Thomas Aquinas to show him his library, took him to his prayer cell where a crucifix hung. The incident is significant in putting first things first. But a look at a sermon that Bonaventura preached would show that he brought to that prayer cell a disciplined mind and spirit that knew the best that the ages could give, and that he brought this with him in order to lay it at the foot of the cross as he knelt to remember the sacrificial love of Jesus.

This in no sense suggests that formal education necessarily cultivates or prepares the spirit for ministry or that the humble spirit-tipped word of an utterly unlearned man or woman or child in a meeting may not minister to its deepest need, but it does propose that nothing is too good for God and that over the years there is no preparation of the mind and heart and will that God cannot use and use with power to further ministry.

As I think of the vocal ministry of two great Quaker spirits of our time, Rufus M. Jones and Henry T. Hodgkin, and of their outward preparation for ministry, I know how they stored their minds and hearts not only first and foremost with the Bible but also with the best books of their generation. Books of poetry, literature, religious history, and especially biography were always on their tables, and Rufus Jones's personal collection of books which are now in the Haverford library are full of heavy pencil markings and marginal notes, showing the intimacy of his encounter with these books. Henry Hodgkin took the first hour each morning for a time of silent prayer, for reading the Bible or some devotional book, and then for writing his heart out in a common-place book that no one ever saw but that enabled him to set down some of the insights that had come to him.

Gratry in an old book called *The Well Springs* speaks of this discipline of listening and writing which Henry Hodgkin practiced.

What, you will ask of me, is the meaning of listening to God? . . . What am I to do in reality? Here is my answer. You are to write. . . . St. Augustine begins his *Soliloquies* thus, "I was a prey to a thousand various thoughts and for many days had been making strenuous efforts to find myself, my own good, and the evil to avoid, when on a sudden . . . it was said to me, 'If you find what you are seeking, what will you do with it? To whom will you confide it?' 'I shall keep it in my memory,' answered I. 'But is your memory capable of treasuring all that your mind has conceived?' 'No, certainly it cannot.' 'Then you must write, that this offspring of your mind may animate and strengthen you!' "

Not only may the storing of the memory, the wide reading, the life of prayer, and the discipline of writing like a well-laid fire in the life of the worshiping minister be consumed in worship, but the worshiper's own faculties are of importance as well. The power of reason to interpret a spiritual insight and put it convincingly is a precious gift. When John Churchman declares, "I let in reasoning, and so departed for a time from my inward guide and safe counsellor," it is well to recall Isaac Penington's classic remark that, "Reason is not sin; but a deviating from that from which reason came is sin." Churchman is referring to precisely this deviating of reason from that from which it came, but the Quaker Quietists generally neglected the more precise distinctions of Penington and denounced the faculty itself.

To learn how to use the full preparation and the full faculties both before and after the inward tendering and the inward accent is, and always must be, the condition of a sound Quaker ministry. Teresa of Avila once wrote, "God gave us our faculties for use; each of them will receive its proper reward. Then do not let us try to charm them to sleep, but permit them to do their work, until divinely called to something higher."[1] When Friedrich von Hügel wrote in the opening lines of the preface to his monumental work *The Mystical Element of Religion* that it "embodies well nigh all that the writer has been able to *learn and to test,* in the matter of religion, during now some thirty years of adult life," he was speaking of what mature Friends who covet a powerful vocal ministry might long to have go with them to meeting and be laid before the flame of waiting silence. For to those who have been seasoned and prepared in this way and who bring with them to meeting all that they have been able to learn and to test in the years of their adult life, there is a mighty instrument and witness which the Listener may freshly anoint and use.

VOCAL MINISTRY AND THE MINISTERING WORSHIPER'S OWN COMMITMENT

Closely related to the prayer and study and the full use of a person's faculties and past experience in the waiting ministry is the depth of the ministering worshiper's own personal religious commitment. For the task of preparing for the Quaker ministry is one of preparing the person and not the message. It is not hard to believe that one of the most effective preparations for ministry is past faithfulness in response to divine leading. If this faithfulness has been tested by times when the person went against personal earthly advantage, it cannot but have left the individual more open, and to have made the fellow worshipers to whom this person ministered more open because they knew the quality of personal commitment.

The amazing itinerant lay ministry of the eighteenth century was carried on only at the heaviest cost to the Friends involved, and to their families. It affected the style of life and the choice of business which would free them from cumber that they might follow where they were inwardly led. The sheer fatigue of months and even years on horseback, the perils to health and the dangers attending travel by land and sea in that period, the long separation from their families, the willingness when widowed even to entrust their own children to others in order to set out dauntlessly on these journeys, was a powerful witness to those with whom they entered the silent worship that these men and women were committed to the Inward Guide and that they cared deeply for the welfare of their souls.

The words of the young wife of Job Scott, the lay minister, tell of one form of this cost in a way that few could miss. As she lay dying she said to him:

> I have several times thought I should have been willing to have taken the care of these dear children a little longer, if it had been the Divine will; and I have thought, if it might have been

so ordered, I could have given up everything that might have been called for; even if it had been to give thee up to travel in truth's service, let the time be longer or shorter. I have always given thee up with a good degree of cheerfulness, and have been supported in thy absence beyond my expectation; and yet I have often thought since thy return from thy last journey, that I did not know that I could ever give thee up again, or bear up in thy absence. But in this sickness I have felt as though I could give up all, if I might be spared a little longer to help along in the care of children. It has seemed to me that I should give thee up, my dear husband, to go wherever the Lord may lead thee; it has seemed so, but maybe it would not be so with me, if I should be tried with it; and perhaps I shall be taken away, that thou mayest be set more at liberty to attend to the Lord's requirings, in whatever part of the word he may see meet to employ thee.[2]

John Churchman having been on a journey in the ministry in Britain, Ireland and Holland records, "In this visit I was from home four years and twelve days, having travelled (on horseback) by land nine thousand one hundred miles and attended about a thousand meetings." On finally landing in Wilmington, Delaware, after this long absence he says, with his characteristic restraint, "I went home that evening, where I found a kind reception."[3]

The equivalent in miniature of this kind of service today by which a concern for the fellow-worshipers of our meetings may lead us to find the necessary time to know them, to visit them, to have them in our homes, and to make their needs our concern is a tested preparation for ministry of the highest importance. A person who throughout the week thinks of the approaching meeting for worship and holds up inwardly some of the needs of those who attend, is being prepared for that kind of participation in the meeting for worship that may open the way for helpful ministry. Ministry is often deepened by our natural exposure to those in greatest need, whether it be physical need, as in a constant visiting of the poor, of those in prison, of those whom group prejudice segregates, or to the poor in spirit, those who face mental turmoil and inner problems. Few who feel this kind of responsible love for the meeting do not in the course of the week find some experience, some insight, something they have read that has helped them, some crushing burden they know some member or some group is bearing which they have held up to the Light, without these things appearing as seeds out of which ministry could grow.

WHAT TURNS THE WAITING WORSHIPER INTO A MINISTER?

But all of this girding up of the worshipers who gather is preparation, and no more. When they enter the meeting, they proceed as any worshiper to open themselves before the Listener. Once William Penn is said to have begun to preach on the way up the aisle, as he was taking his seat in meeting. But for a message truly to come up out of a meeting for worship, it must have been held in its inner tempering power. While it is not a matter of time, few meetings can gather in less than a quarter of an hour and some find it takes at least twice that long before a deep level is reached. Tempered ministry, then, must rise out of a gathered meeting, and it is not surprising that it seldom comes until after this gathering has taken place.

What happens that turns the worshiper into a minister? The worshiper may have brought certain seeds out of which ministry could flower or may have come without any expectation of that day being called into the ministry. What the worshiper is and what moves inside the worshiper is slowly disclosed before the living Listener, who gathers the meeting into the presence, and there in that tendering presence an ordering takes place.

The worshiper may and often does feel that all that was brought to the meeting is not in the tide that is running or instead may feel that something that had seemed important has now become enormously more important but in quite a fresh way. The worshiper's mind may be drawn to this in such a way as to see its implications for personal life with an icy clarity, and the individual consequences may be all too apparent. Should such a personal message then, be shared with the meeting? It may be, but this is not necessarily the case. Much is given us for our own use and testing before it is given us to publish as truth.

Job Scott says so simply, "I was shut up as to words but had clear openings. It is sometimes wisely ordered, that precious and divine openings are treasured up in the Lord's treasury: but how dangerous would it be . . . to lavish them out among people only because we are favoured with opening without the word of command, to deliver them to people."[4] John Churchman, too, relates, "I began to see there was a difference between seeing what was to be done, and being bidden to do the thing shown . . . being made sensible that every opening or vision which the Lord is pleased to manifest to his servants is not for immediate utterance."[5]

I have yet to see the time when some moving insight that came into a worshiper's mind in meeting but that was not suitable for immediate sharing was ever lost. For if it goes into the life of the worshiper it will bear the ultimate fruit in that worshiper's faithful preparation for later ministry, and if it is meant for the meeting but seems at this time to lack the compulsion to be publicly shared, it is sure to gather strength and power and one day be drawn forward when it is in the life and to be charged with added strength for having been held back at the Listener's disposal.

In another person, however, there may be an accent placed on something that has grown up in the mind in worship and a great tenderness rise up in the worshiper toward those that are gathered in worship. This may grow until the worshiper feels a deep sense of the inward need to which this message that is springing up within might speak. As in John Woolman's call to visit the Indians on the Susquehanna, so in genuine ministry, "Love was the first motion." John Churchman writes how in his experience the call to vocal ministry came: "As I sat in one of our meetings, I felt a flow of affection to the people . . . in which extraordinary flow of affection I had a bright opening."[6]

This inward caring for those to whom one is to minister and this inward disclosure of conditions and of need is a most important part of the preparation to speak. For in that moment of being drawn into speech by the Listener, the opaque veil that separates us from each other in so much of life seems swiftly to be lifted as this life and power courses through us.

WHERE WORDS COME FROM

The insight that has come must be clothed. The early Christians were counseled to "take no thought for what you are to say," and there are often times when in a flash all is ready. Illustrations are there and the words with which to begin and to close this exercise in the ministry have all unbidden tumbled into place. Far more often however the message grows, and in the growing, the worshipers experience the most creative moments of their lives.

Count Keyserling declares somewhere that all of the luminous insights one ever gets in one's life can be cupped into a few fractions of a second. But in a gathered meeting this miracle may happen countless times in a single life. In the company of the Divine Listener and of the silent worshiping community, the worshiping minister sees a focusing take place and sees nonessentials trimmed away. Arnold Toynbee once criticized a sketch which his mother had drawn, complaining that she had omitted some foreground detail that his eye could see in the scene that she had drawn. She replied that in sketching, the first principle one had to learn was what to leave out. Here this operation of what to leave out takes place without effort. A hidden meaning that at first disclosed only a part of itself, and the least important part, now may be drawn forward; an example falls into place; a verse one had not recalled for years; a confirmation of scripture that is unmistakable are all there.

In this very moment a worshiper is more passive and more alive; more in the spell of Another, yet more intensely existing as self; more a living cell of the worshiping group, and yet more of a separated organ cut off in order that the worshiper may speak to its condition than the worshiper can believe could be true. When this centering process has done its work there is a gathering of compulsion that the message should be given. In some, this compulsion heightens the breathing and is as inwardly perceptible as any physical arousal of adrenalin in its preparation of the body for action. On others it is a quieter compulsion that goes on at the mental level. If this is steadily resisted, the compulsion may fade, but the worshiper is not likely to escape the sense of infidelity to the call that came, and restless days may follow.

In his *Faith of a Quaker,* John William Graham has dared to set down with admirable frankness the experience of a mature Quaker in being drawn into ministry in a meeting. The long paragraph is so revealing that no sound account of this exercise could well omit it:

> It comes by waiting. When I sit down in meeting I recall whatever may have struck me freshly during the past week. This is, initially at least, a voluntary and outward act. It means simply that the outward man is ready to run if he is sent. It means that the will is given up to service; and it is quite possible to stop everything and take an opposite attitude. So thoughts suggest themselves—a text that has smitten one during the week—a new light on a phrase, a verse of poetry— some incident private or public. These pass before the door whence shines the heavenly light. Are they transfigured? Sometimes, yes; sometimes, no. If nothing flames, silence is my portion. I turn from ideas of the ministry to my own private needs. From these sometimes a live coal from off the altar is brought, suddenly and unexpectedly and speech follows. Sometimes it does not. Again there are times when the initial thought strikes in of itself from the Inner Man beyond the will. These are times to be thankful for. Often two or three thoughts that have struck home during the week are woven together in unexpected ways. When the fire is kindled, the blaze is not long. In five minutes from its inception the sermon is there, the heart beats strongly and up the man must get. How trying is any interruption during those few rapt and fruitful minutes, when the whole scheme is unfolding itself, and flashing itself upon the brain. There are the five or six main points, the leading sentences of thought are there, the introductory ex- pository teaching, the generalization, the illustration, the final lesson and appeal, they fall into place. The sermon is made, but I, the slow compiler, did not make it.[7]

The content of this ministry can never be prescribed from without. There is no Quaker liturgical cycle of the Christian year. Yet it can be said that a meeting whose members read and inwardly digest the Bible, who pray, and who are exposed to the needs of one another and of those who suffer in the world around them will not fail to be drawn down into the great Christian theme of the love, the joy, and the greatness of God; of suffering, sin, redemption, atonement, and resurrection. The passionate new interest among younger Friends today in Christian theology has come in part because these great themes have been too much neglected in the Quaker recent past. But this fresh accent on theology will not be enough. I recall how Agnes Tierney once told of passing a bookshop in Philadelphia and noting a sign in the window which read "Second-hand theology for sale." It will only be when these great themes come up out of a baptism of inner experience that they will speak to the needs of meetings for worship in our time. Only then can they help to lift and frame all that we do.

The content of these messages when it is authentic fulfills the requirements of existential preaching. It exposes to light, demolishes, and makes uninhabitable for the future comfortable hollow logs where we had long been snugly hibernating. I remember hearing of how the schoolmaster in Le Chambon, at a farewell dinner for André Trocmé who was leaving his long pastorate there, described their previous two fine pastors who had been able to give them weekly sermons to which, he insisted, one could really look forward. After them you could go home and enjoy a big Sunday dinner. But in 1934, Pastor Trocmé came and changed all that. Since then he had never, not for a single Sunday, been permitted to leave the church in complacent content with himself. "I see the wrong that round me lies, I feel the guilt within," wrote Whittier, and existential preaching touches this spring in us. To interpret the tireless and utterly adequate reconciling love of the One who stands at the door and knocks, to move the springs of human compassion, to take away fear and restore vulnerable love is content enough to sustain any worshiping group.

In the preparation of a worshiper to minister, the influence of the corporate waiting, of the worshiping group, is not a small one. Those physically sensitive Quietist members were often silent in meeting after meeting because they felt a darkness in the group that stifled them. Job Scott wrote of such an experience, "I was enabled to sound an alarm among them." A worshiping group that contains a number of persons who are in a state of lassitude and torpor, in a condition of numbness induced by the dispersed character of their ordinary living, in a condition of exclusive absorption in their own internal problems, or in a state of critical testiness toward each other and toward anyone who may speak does not fulfill the requirements of positive collective expectancy out of which real worship and real ministry may come.

A medical doctor once refused to give a bedridden college professor patient of his a most helpful book saying that it would serve no purpose, because he would only tear it to pieces with his critically poised mind. For every plant there is a degree of frost beyond which it will winter-kill, and the tender plant of vocal ministry is no exception. It is when the worshiping group is open and loving, it is when it is abandoned to the inner exercise that may take place in it, when there is a movement at its heart expressed in Guy Butler's lines, "We wait, we wait the catalyst, we wait, we wait, we wait," that it becomes possible for one member to arise and express the very moving which half a dozen others may have felt, albeit not in their own words. In such an atmosphere when ministry is brief and does not try to exhaust the insight, others may rise and add to it until something grows that no single speaker could have presented, and the meeting closes with a feeling of blessing and unity.

How blessed any Protestant minister might feel if given the privilege of sitting for an hour in silent waiting with a little inner company of the congregation that week. How that message might be clipped, how it might be refocused, and upon occasion how it might be completely recast as the minister was swept by a deeper sense of both the need of the group and of the abundance of God's power to meet the need. In such an experience, how it might be charged with power!

How helpful, too, it might be if this occasion might become a regular spring and source of ministry, if ministry were required of the Protestant minister that week, or a place where one of the lay group might from time to time be inwardly drawn to discharge the vocal ministry of the meeting and on that occasion relieve the minister of that exercise. If to this little group could in time be added the whole congregation who would all gather with the minister to wait in this way, with the freedom to minister shared still more widely, and the message come straight from a freshly touched mind and heart, is it impossible to see some, at least, of the steps by which this Quaker treasure of a silent waiting ministry could be shared with the whole free church family?

QUAKER WORSHIP AND THE UNFOLDING OF CONCERNS

But the experience of worship and of ministry has not done its full work until there is a kind of inner "regrouping of one's resources," as Gabriel Marcel so effectively expresses it, until in the life of the worshiper there is produced a state of *disponibilité*, a condition of being expendable, of being at the disposal of the Listener and of one's fellows who are infinitely precious to one. This tendering of the heart and being drawn into a fresh sensitiveness to the needs of others, this malleable willingness to be used in meeting that need is the condition in which what Friends have called a "concern" may arise.

The word "concern" is often used too lightly today. Friends may refer to any whim or fancy of an individual to do some act or to champion some cause as that person's "concern." In its truest form, a concern refers to a costly inner leading to some act that in the course of its fulfillment may take over the very life of the one it engages. At this level, it can be said that in a genuine concern, a person has been drawn into the living inward linkage of individual and God, of individual and individual, and of individual and creation. For to be brought into a condition of awareness of the compassion of the living Listener is to have disclosed to the worshiper a realization of the redemptive order of love that girdles our world for its healing. Is it surprising then that men and women who have been listened into life should be called upon not only to serve as a delicate litmus solution to record and point to outer and inner needs, but should be drawn as well to set about the process of meeting the needs that they or others have detected?

This does not mean to depreciate those exercises of worship and ministry which culminate in stirring the level of being of the worshipers themselves. This result is more than ample justification for them. But it does imply that when the Listener who has been revealed by Jesus Christ changes the level of our being, Friends over the centuries have found an accompanying passion of love and concern for their fellow creatures that has not remained vague and abstract but has frequently drawn them into specific and concrete expressions of it.

The order of the unfolding of a concern has not been identical. Occasionally the concern has put its finger on a specific thing to be done and on the initial steps of carrying it out. When Joseph Sturge in his inner agony over the steadily worsening relations of England and Russia and the impending Crimean War felt personally drawn to visit the Czar and to labor with him, the concern and the means seemed clear and specific. More often the concern has laid hold of the person in terms of a deep inner distress over the wrongness of some situation or a yearning to minister to some condition of need without more than the first minute step being clear as to how to deal with it. A person may have a leading to go or to offer to go to some situation of need. One may go and remain there for some time, and perhaps when one has returned may go again before the specific steps to be taken become clear. If the first step that is laid upon a person is not undertaken, the later ones are not disclosed. As Adrienne von Speyr says in her commentary on the Gospel of John, "It is hardly ever possible to see from the start all that God is to mean to one . . . Once open to the light, he may ask God to claim him more essentially and more profoundly. But on one condition, that he does not refuse the first small act God demands of him."

"The first small act" is sooner or later known to every worshiper. The first act may be a visit, or a letter, or a gift, or it may be a first alert to clear the decks of one's engagements for orders that are still sealed. The mysterious thing of it all is that in God's eyes there are no "little" things. Everything matters and everything leads to something further. Even when a concern is as specific as Joseph Sturge's, the disclosure is still progressive. How little he knew at that time the humiliation and misunderstanding that his journey to Russia was to cost him in the months and years of patriotic fervor that came with the Crimean War. How little he could foresee that out of that humiliation and inward chastening was to come his call to Finland to release a chain of reconciliation that has not yet fully spent its force.

The revisions to major concerns which subsequent reflection or the wise provision of the Quaker requirement that these concerns be laid before a gathered meeting for their counsel and acceptance, or which the measured judgment of wise Friends who may be personally consulted may make to help shape the course of a concern has in practice been found only to result in refining it. If the delay entailed by this process of scrutiny should whittle the concern away to nothing and it should wither in the mind of the one on whom it was laid, then its authenticity can be viewed with considerable suspicion. For a genuine concern is marked both by its persistence and, strangely enough, by its flexibility and openness about the means by which it is to be carried out.

Meister Eckhart's remark that "a man can only spend in good works what he earns in contemplation" is not unconnected with the Society of Friends' experience in the matter of concerns out of which its acts of service have risen. For only as these services have sprung from and been shaped and consummated in the life of such inward concerns have they left any lasting residue that has quickened people to the love of God and their fellows and to an implementing of vital peace. For that reason our times call Friends to a fresh season of inward waiting on the Divine Listener who can alone draw out and redispose of our tightly clutched lives and our personal and institutional plans and programs.

The Society's experience, however, has been that those who from the first entry into a concern have learned to listen, have learned to keep open, have asked the question about each turn of events, "What may I learn from this? What has this to teach me about the way I am now to go?" have been the ones whom nothing could deter, and have had operating in them a process of correction which did not fail them in any situation that arose. The faith in the accessibility of the Divine Listener that has marked the carrying out of Quaker concerns and the subsequent listening temper with its flexibility and openness to admit error and to correct it has had a cleansing effect upon the diseases of private fanaticism that may readily infect such action. This openness to continual correction has had the practical effect of revealing to many who followed a concern how brittle and fragile was the thread of their commitment when they undertook it and how far the Divine Listener had used this concern to draw them on into the divine redemptive action and to cleanse and clarify them, a process that worship alone had only begun. For our action like our words is being listened to not only by our fellows but by the Eternal One, and it is only as we feel that One's scrutiny and respond to that One's illumination in what we do that we become a part of the redemptive circle that longs to draw not only all humanity but all creation into its healing power.

NOTES

1. Teresa of Avila, *The Interior Castle,* 4:3.
2. Job Scott, *Journal* (London, 1815), 284-85.
3. John Churchman, *An Account of Gospel Labors* (Philadelphia, 1882), 189.
4. Ibid., 137.
5. Ibid., 52, 196.
6. Ibid., 137.
7. John William Graham, *The Faith of a Quaker* (London: Cambridge, 1920), 245-46.

THE TWENTY-THIRD PSALM AND THE DIALECTIC OF RENEWAL

"The Twenty-Third Psalm and the Dialectic of Renewal" is an undisguised religious message, which was originally given in a religious service in Bay View, Michigan. It seems suitable to conclude this little collection of Gleanings *with the psalmist's witness to the Shepherd's undergirding support of us as we face the blows that come our way.*

I suppose that there is no psalm that we all regard with such respect and affection as the Twenty-third Psalm. A small boy who was learning it started off with his version of the first line: "The Lord is my Shepherd, that's all I want"; he was not far from the heart of the matter. Each of us has snatches of that psalm that come back to us in the crises of life, snatches that repeat themselves in our minds in the sleepless hours. I want to explore two of these that have meant much to me. The first is, "He maketh me to lie down." And the second is, "He restoreth my soul." These are not statements of creed or of dogma, but are instead the Jewish psalmist's reports of personal experience out of the depths of life's turbulent struggle. For me, these experiences are not things that happened some three thousand years ago but are experiences that take place again and again in our lives today if we will attend to their promises and be willing to yield to them.

These two confessions out of the psalmist's depths belong together, for there are few of us who can have our souls restored until we have been brought to lie down. Clover seed has to be scarified, driven over sharp, sandpaper-like surfaces that break open the hull, before it germinates well when planted in the earth. We human beings seem to require the same treatment, and life does not hesitate to provide it.

Florence Allshorn, a British saint of a generation ago, had returned from a stiff missionary assignment in Uganda with tuberculosis that, while ultimately healed, prevented her return to Africa. She spent the years after her recovery teaching prospective missionaries in a training college in Britain until it became clear to her that theoretical instruction prior to some baptism by fire in the mission field itself was unreal and ineffective. As she put it, "They have not yet come to the end of themselves." Instead of teaching, she set up a rural hostel in Sussex called St. Julian's, where missionaries, weary and "torn open" by work in the field, could live for a sizable part of their furloughs. She also drew together a small sisterhood of committed women who would minister to the spiritual needs of these "broken open" veterans.

How much the same it is with us all. Until life compels us to come to the end of ourselves and to stop, often to be shattered, to be searched in our most mysterious depths, even to be taken beyond the possibility of coming to terms with our new situation by our own means; until life pushes us out into depths where we cannot, hard as we may try, touch bottom with our feet, there is little likelihood of our turning to the mysterious Other, the one the psalmist calls Lord and our Shepherd, for the restoration of our souls.

Even a hard-driven psychotherapist like Carl G. Jung had no doubt that the Shepherd is always present. He went as far as to have an inscription placed over the doorway of his consulting room which read, "Whether he is called upon or whether he is not called upon, God will be present." But when life is smoothly going along according to plan, especially when it is according to our own plan, how easy it is to forget either the Restorer or the need for restoration. It is only when God appears in the role of disturber that "He maketh me to lie down" in some peak experience in life that we have at least a moment of openness again to the presence of the mysterious Restorer.

When I speak of God as the disturber in the business of "He maketh me to lie down," I am not suggesting some kind of spiritual determinism that charges God with initiating each action that we perform or that affects us. Neither you nor I know enough about human freedom, about the relative autonomies of the different facets of life, and about the operation of divine providence to dare to charge God with causing some specific act of intervention in order to bring us low and lower our thresholds to a new awareness of God's healing, restoring presence. Neither do we know enough, however, to exclude utterly God's profound and continuous involvement in our lives! Perhaps it is enough to say what W. H. Auden says, "It is where we are wounded that God speaks to us."

I used psychologist Maslow's well-known phrase in referring to "peak experiences" that profoundly affect us if we do not ignore them. These peak experiences can be moments of ecstasy or they can be moments of being shattered and humiliated. It is these latter shattering peaks that we are concerned with here. A woman at Wainwright House in Rye, New York, told a group of us about the first time she had heard of these "peak experiences" and about her husband's looking over her shoulder and chuckling over her writing the words "peek experiences." This seems to me to be an example of an inspired misunderstanding. When I am laid low, when I am made to lie down in life and, seeking meaning for my life from this unsolicited and unwanted position I am suddenly given a whole new angle of vision on my life and its priorities, how better could this be described than as a peek into the real nature of things—a peek into the mysterious abyss in me that underlies the well-grooved "everything under control" surface of my life? If I will go deeper into this experience, I have the possibility of the recovery of even a "peek" into the never-slumbering presence in me of the One that the psalmist bears witness to in the line, "He restoreth my soul."

Let us look at a few examples of these times of being made to lie down, at these peeks into the abyss of life when I am no longer adequate, and at these peeks into the way that the promised restoration, if it is not evaded or neglected, may heal me and may launch my life on a new level.

He maketh me to lie down. I have a German Quaker friend who has been a surgeon in Africa for over twenty-five years. His first assignment there was in western Kenya. When I visited him in 1953 at the mission hospital to which he was attached, I found him seething with revolt at the narrowness of the evangelical religion and the smallness of outlook that he found among his American colleagues, most of whom had come from a semi-rural, midwestern background in Indiana. More recently, he sent me the first portion of his autobiography and entrusted it to me to look over for him. In the manuscript I found an account of a "peek" experience that had come to him shortly after my early visit.

He had been brought back to Indiana to the headquarters of the religious group that ran the mission hospital. In the course of his visit, he spent the night in the home of one of those narrow, limited, evangelically-oriented church members of the group under which he was working in Africa. His host's wife was a polio victim in a wheelchair; the husband and their six children had to pitch in and do the housework, but there was never a murmur of complaint. The host himself was a foreman in a small factory in the town. After supper, he took my surgeon friend out to a shed behind the house and explained how, since God had come into his life, he had always longed to be a missionary and had felt especially the pull to work in western Kenya. Since he knew that he had no special skill that would be useful there and because of his wife's condition and his large family, it was clear that he could never himself go to help. Instead, he had saved his money and, with a sizable loan that he was still paying off, he had bought a bulldozer, which he showed to my friend out there in the shed. He explained that after he had come home from his factory work and eaten his supper, he was able to get in two, three, or four hours of work with the bulldozer and, after paying off his monthly payment on the loan, he had been able to send about two hundred dollars each month to the mission board as his contribution to the work of the hospital. My friend suddenly realized that this amount added up, almost to the dollar, to what he received at that time as his mission salary. He understood that he was actually being carried and permitted to do the work in surgery that he loved by this humble, unassuming evangelical midwestern Christian! For this German surgeon, it was a "peek" experience that searched to the core his fastidiousness, his contempt, his resentments, and his sense of superiority. *He maketh me to lie down. He restoreth my soul.*

I was reading recently in my journal from 1947-48, a time when Dorothy and I were in prostrate Germany in Quaker service, and I came across a passage that I had translated from a German article by Gertrud von le Fort, a Roman Catholic novelist of great stature, which described what the war and the bombings and the Hitler-dominated situation within Germany felt like in the closing years of the war. There was a caption over the passage that I copied that read: *"Was bleibt wenn alles versinkt?"* (What remains when all is blotted out?) Gertrud von le Fort wrote, as I translated:

> Certainly we believed in God before. But what does trust in God mean as one lives in a well-ordered state, with dependable police protection, with money, prosperity and careful plans? I assure you it is quite otherwise with trust in God if all that gives human assurance falls away and one must say at any moment, not only symbolically but actually, that the roof may fall over my head. At any moment all that is precious and beloved and that I cannot live without may be swept away. If I am ill tomorrow, there is no hospital to take me in. You can be turned into the street at any moment. You can be transported for days or weeks in a cattle car bedded with straw and with no roof. You can freeze, and you freeze. You can starve, and you starve. You can be subjected to the most painful and gruesome death without guilt on your part or without any possibility of defending yourself. Any day you can get word that your dearest friends or relations have been buried in their towns by an attack or that they have died in the gas chamber of a concentration camp—at any moment the same may be your own fate.

After this she returned to her basic question, "What remains?" Her answer was decisive, "When church doors shut, the sacrament is not able to be given out, liturgy and preaching are silenced and the church is in ashes and rubble—God remains, Christ remains—and that is an unspeakable comfort in the midst of the world's breakup." *He maketh me to lie down. He restoreth my soul.*

I had a friend named Thomas Sugrue who, at the height of his career as a writer and a sharer of deep insights, was treated at the Johns Hopkins University Hospital for what seemed a minor ailment. Due to some medical miscalculation, he was permanently paralyzed from the neck down so that he became utterly dependent upon others for his every need. He lived on for some eight years after this incident. His sharing with us of what this dependence meant in the way of self-disclosure and the overcoming of fear and the letting go to the heart of things to the Shepherd left none of us who knew him in those years untouched. *He maketh me to lie down. He restoreth my soul.* Our library of devotional books at Wainwright House has been named for Thomas Sugrue because he was one who was made to lie down and who discovered all afresh the power of the Shepherd "who restoreth my soul."

Recently in Stockholm was celebrated the one hundredth anniversary of the birth of Emelia Fogelklou Norlind, a Swedish Quaker woman of the spirit who left few that she touched the same. In the middle thirties of this century, she had a serious operation during which her heart stopped. For some minutes the doctors worked over her and with what was then daring adrenalin therapy, they got the heart beating again and brought her back to life. She said to me when I saw her shortly after her recovery, "You know, Douglas, since my recent death things look very different. Many things that before seemed to me of much importance now seem to matter so little, and simple things that before I did not bother about now seem to matter terribly." For a period in her life after this event, she lived near Hogfors in central Sweden. Two days a week she went to a room that the commune secured for her and just stayed there during the day for talk with anyone who wanted to see her. She was not a medical doctor; she was not a therapist; she was a human being open to talk sensitively and listeningly with other flesh and blood human beings, and there was always a waiting list of those who wanted to see her. *He maketh me to lie down. He restoreth my soul.*

Martin Buber tells in his *Between Man and Man* of how his whole approach to dialogue, which was one of his major contributions, began. A young man came one day to ask him some searching questions and Buber answered them routinely in what he regarded as a competent manner. The student went away and took his own life. *He maketh me to lie down.* Buber from that moment on knew that he must be *there* to each person who came to him and give to that person his complete and open attention. He understood that nothing less would ever again be adequate. *He restoreth my soul.*

Several years ago a close friend of mine who had returned to this country to become the president of a prominent theological seminary in Chicago and was completely absorbed in the limitless duties of his new post was brought low when his sixteen-year-old daughter secretly drew all the money out of her bank account, took a change of clothes, and unequivocally ran away. For almost a month no one could find her. The disappearance got into the papers and day and night phone calls from deranged persons suggested all kinds of false clues and horrible possibilities. The daughter was eventually found and returned home unscathed. Soon afterwards her father sent out a letter to his close friends confessing what this experience had meant to him and to his wife.

In the letter he told how the experience had confronted their own specious image of themselves as caring parents and as perhaps role models of a Christian family. He spoke also of a whole new level of understanding of their beloved daughter who suffered quietly but acutely from her father's over-busyness and preoccupation and who resented their new life. This life brought drastic limitations to her movements in a great city like Chicago in contrast to the utter freedom that she had in a relatively medium-sized community in Switzerland. Out of the terrific pain and humiliation of this shattering of their self-images had come a whole new level of inward yielding and of understanding in the family of each other and of themselves. It was clear that they had got the message that was pinned on this event in their lives and that had been brought into a further dimension and a clearer focus of the costliness of real love. *He maketh me to lie down. He restoreth my soul.*

I have mentioned a few of the occasions in which "peek" experiences have come to persons and in which, from the abyss of humiliation and weakness, these persons have been made to lie down in their own strength and have by yielding been brought to discover what remains. They have had their souls restored by the Shepherd of life to whom they were, in their trouble, made open. Each reader could go on with ever so many more such instances. A person commits some sin that ruins a career; a person slips into an addiction to alcohol or drugs or hardness of heart; our loved ones become the victims of some wandering germ and are gone and life closes in on us; a business merger forces someone out of a job at a scarcely reemployable age; we fail a child; we teach a class badly; we fail to listen to what our wife or our husband is trying in so many indirect languages to tell us, and the relationship is suddenly severed.

We have seen what these persons we looked at did when *they* were compelled to lie down. What do *we* do? How do *we* react? We can fall into a wallow of self-pity and resentment at life's brutality and ask why this should happen to us. We can plunge into despair and regard ourselves as hopeless, as worthy of perpetual self-hate and perhaps consider suicide as the only way to settle the matter. We can falsify the facts and try to find ways to deceive ourselves. We can justify ourselves to ourselves by comparisons with others. After all, we are no worse than others. Seventy percent of our fellow citizens are said to cheat somewhere on their income taxes! We dredge up some word about ourselves that seems exonerating. Søren Kierkegaard calls this "flight into the crowd." For him the crowd is the hiding place from God where we can be lulled into learning nothing from our experiences, from having been brought low, from having been made to lie down. In our Western society there is another more widely used and still more widely-approved-of method of dealing with these situations. It is to ride them out, to become stoical, and to toughen up inside and wait for them to pass. There is a story of a meeting of Metternich and Guizot in which Metternich tells Guizot that in his own long career as a foreign minister of Austria he has never made a mistake. Guizot is said to have replied that he had been more fortunate, for in his long career as a foreign minister of France he had frequently been mistaken but he had never been unseated by it! To brazen it through is a possible response. But it is not the deepest response, it is not the Christian response, and it is not the reponse that in the ultimate situation of death is any longer possible.

When I am made to lie down in life's unfolding, I am being given another chance, if I only could know it. For when I am made to lie down, when my public image is shattered, when my assurance of health and strength and companionship from those I love most is cut off, when I may even have lost the very image of my own destiny in my falling and my failure, I may be given a peek into the very womb of God where a rebirth is possible, where a fresh regrouping of all that my life has been suddenly comes into focus. This does not mean that I shall be restored to where I was or that I may not have been bidden to a condition that I am quite unable to reverse. But there is even such a thing as dying inwardly healed, and there is such a thing as the Inward Restorer's giving me again a peek into the image of what my life is really meant to be both in this life and beyond. I may long since have lost or blurred this image and now I find that the Restorer, the Shepherd, has kept it and has returned it to me, all radiant with its luminous, beckoning power in the abyss of my despair. *He restoreth my soul.*

Once again Auden's line returns: "It is where we are wounded that God speaks to us." In my extremity, the peek into the real way that my life has always been lured to take gives me a new angle of vision. If I do not evade it or ignore it; if I face it, make a clean breast of it to God and to those most intimately affected by it, I come to know what the psalmist meant by the line "He restoreth my soul." I rise in the morning and instead of wondering how I can get through this day or this week or this month as quickly as possible, to get it behind me, to get it over with, a new sense of wonder is born and I look expectantly at the day, at what fresh things it will bring, at what hidden newness it will reveal for me to respond to. In his *Confessions,* Tolstoy talks of the difference in his life after such a peek experience in 1876. He compares it to going hurriedly into a city full of urgent business and then suddenly the business is seen not to be urgent at all. With an easy mind he turns round and starts quietly homewards again and what was on the left hand is now on the right and what was on the right hand is now on the left. If I am attentive and willing this can happen not once in life but again and again in the process of continuous conversion.

Emily Morgan, who founded the little Episcopal order for women living in the world that is called the Companions of the Holy Cross, brings to us the psalmist's "He maketh me to lie down" and "He restoreth my soul" so freshly. In a letter written late in her life, she speaks to us of how as a girl, after she had said her prayers for the family, including the dog and the pony, and the lights had been put out, there came a beautiful human hand outlined with heavenly light out of the darkness, and to my childish mind it was the Hand of God. Into it I put everything that I could think of. I can smile now at the variety very much like the contents of a little boy's pocket—my sins, my joys and my small worries, the most absurd little things and I touched with absolute confidence that Hand. . . . Once I touched a wound print, and then I cried until our Lord told me to turn over and go to sleep. I often do the same thing now, and the things I place there are just as queer as when I was little. I often think they must make my guardian angel smile.

The hand with the wound print is still there to restore. When all else is swept away, when life itself is swept away, God remains, Christ remains, the wounded hand is still extended to hold me firm. Rendall Harris, a British Quaker scholar and man of the spirit, was asked one time by a woman what death was really like. He confessed that death for him was still an impenetrable mystery, but he was utterly confident of one thing about it, which was that it would be a personally conducted tour! *He maketh me to lie down. He restoreth my soul.*

Douglas V. Steere is recognized as an authority on the centered and comtemplative spiritual life. He has published many books and articles including *Doors into Life, Together in Solitude, Quaker Spirituality,* and a translation of Søren Kierkegaard's *Purity of Heart.*

Dr. Steere's interests have always mingled the contemplative and the active life. His extensive travels for the American Friends Service Committee and the Friends World Committee have taken him to Germany, Scandanavia, Britain, Africa, India, and the Orient—literally around the world. Dr. Steere and his wife Dorothy live in Haverford, Pennsylvania, where he is the T. Wistar Brown Professor of Philosophy Emeritus at Haverford College.